A Creative Approach to Teaching Calculation

A Creative Approach to Teaching Calculation

The what, why and how of teaching calculation and number in context

by Josh Lury

BLOOMSBURY

LONDON • NEW DELHI • NEW YORK • SYDNEY

Bloomsbury Education

An imprint of Bloomsbury Publishing Plc

50 Bedford Square	1385 Broadway
London	New York
WC1B 3DP	NY 10018
UK	USA

www.bloomsbury.com

Bloomsbury is a registered trade mark of Bloomsbury Publishing Plc

First published 2015

British Library Cataloguing-in-Publication Data
A catalogue record for this book is available from the British Library.

ISBN: PB: 978-1-4729-1947-2
ePub: 978-1-4729-1937-3
ePDF: 978-1-4729-1936-6

Library of Congress Cataloging-in-Publication Data
A catalog record for this book is available from the Library of Congress.

10 9 8 7 6 5 4 3 2 1

Typeset by Newgen Knowledge Works (P) Ltd., Chennai, India
Printed by CPI Group (UK) Ltd, Croydon, CRO 4YY

This book is produced using paper that is made from wood grown in
managed, sustainable forests. It is natural, renewable and recyclable.
The logging and manufacturing processes conform to the environmental
regulations of the country of origin.

To view more of our titles please visit www.bloomsbury.com

Contents

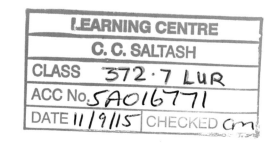

Introduction		1
Some myths and misconceptions		2
How to use this book		2
Types of activity		3
1	A Sense of Number	5
	Getting a feel for number	5
	Taking an interest in number	9
	Patterns in number	11
	Understanding that pattern is the basis of all calculation	12
	Classroom environment	14
	Mathematical stamina and esteem – maths as an emotional activity	19
2	Mastery of Three Key Models	23
	Moving from using objects to mental strategies	23
	Harnessing the power of 100 squares	24
	What's the same and what's different?	24
	Pattern	26
	Counting and moving	27
	Using versus learning	28
	Quick sketches	30
	100 square variations	31
	Harnessing the power of number lines	34
	Hidden assumptions and misconceptions	35
	Ordinality and cardinality	37
	Using versus learning	39
	A physical sense of number lines	40
	Drawing number lines usefully	42
	Jumping on and jumping back	44
	How far from x to y?	47
	Choosing your 'stop-offs'	47
	Zooming in…an infinity of numbers	48
	Harnessing the power of arrays	48
	What do we mean by arrays?	49
	Using arrays to understand number	50

	An efficient method of counting	51
	Arrays and areas	53
3	Four Operations	55
	What is important about learning calculation?	55
	Why do we learn them in pairs?	56
	Are subtraction and division more challenging to learn?	56
	Multiple solutions and more challenging missing information	58
	Addition and subtraction	59
	Decimal place value	62
	Inverse operations (addition and subtraction)	64
	Column addition and subtraction	65
	Complements to…10, 100, 1000…	70
	Making adjustments	70
	Find the difference	71
	Method of equivalent difference	73
	Understanding the difference between addition and multiplication	75
	Double and half	77
	Grouping and sharing	78
	Inverse operations (division and multiplication)	79
	Multiplication chains	81
	Grid method	82
	Flexible partitioning	83
	Column multiplication	85
	Long and short division	87
	Alternative methods	88
4	Decimals and Fractions	91
	Common decimal misconceptions	91
	Decimal remainders	92
	Fraction calculations	94
	Addition and subtraction of fractions	94
	Multiplication and division of fractions	95
	Fractions and division	96
	Further mathematical thinking	97
	Always, sometimes, never true	98
	Always, sometimes, never statements about consecutive numbers	100
	Afterword	103
	Index	105

Introduction

This book is called *A Creative Approach to Calculation*. What is a creative approach and why calculation?

A creative approach is about:

1. Developing a physical and visual intuition about number,
2. Encouraging pupils to forge links between their ideas and develop conceptual understanding,
3. Capturing pupils' curiosity and innate logical reasoning.

The ideas in this book are designed to be rich and engaging but very simple to implement. The creativity is in the approach to number and the harnessing of pattern. There is no need to spend hours making complicated resources – many of the activities require only pencil and paper.

This book is built around five strong core values:

- Calculation is a gateway to outstanding learning for pupils in mathematics.
- Conceptual understanding is important for all pupils.
- All pupils are valued as mathematicians – they are the centre of their own learning.
- Mathematics can be taught in a physically, visually and conceptually rich way for all pupils.
- All pupils and teachers can enjoy maths more, find it more interesting, and develop their mathematical esteem.

This book will show you how pupils can learn more than just how to *use* calculation methods – they will learn *why* and *how* they work. So, just as many of us (I include myself in this list!) can drive a car without knowing what all the components are and do, we are left in a pickle as soon as it breaks down or an unknown warning light comes on. The ideas in this book will help teachers and pupils to look 'under the bonnet' in order to understand how the engine works, how to tune it and how to borrow parts to make other engines work too!

It is very easy to feel disenfranchised by mathematics – as if you are having maths 'done' to you. Mathematics is a vast and ancient subject. Numbers are infinite. Mathematical symbols scrawled across a lecture theatre can appear cold, arcane, and even threatening. One key aim of this book is *to put the pupil at the centre of their own mathematics*: having and testing ideas, manipulating numbers flexibly in order to make them do what they want them to do, making connections and bouncing back from mistakes. The pupils become the mathematicians, and they shape the maths around them.

The approach is to give pupils a sense of mathematical empowerment. It would be impossible to force everyone to love the subject as I do, but I want to help pupils feel that they can achieve, investigate and enjoy the challenges posed by mathematics. And then I hope more people will like maths more than they might have done before, and its joys and beauties will be shared by more human beings!

Some myths and misconceptions

'I was never any good at maths.'

You will have heard this sentence, or perhaps said it yourself; it is a belief held by many adults. Some say it with a sense of shame, some wear it as a badge of honour, many are glad they never have to look at a maths textbook ever again. For some adults, even some who feel they *were* good at maths at school, the idea of being given a maths question to answer on the spot prompts a fear-reaction and a sense of being judged. Not all adults feel like this but a great many do.

Ask yourself:

- What would you like your pupils to say about themselves in relation to maths? What if you asked them this tomorrow? What about in twenty years' time?
- Ask your friends, family or colleagues: "Are you good at maths? How do you know?"
- Ask your pupils the subtly different question: "When do people do their best maths? When do they do their worst maths? How do you think professional mathematicians do maths?"

'The thing about maths is, it's either right or wrong.'

It is difficult to imagine someone developing an interest in maths despite always getting the wrong answer. It's unlikely you will overhear someone saying "Oh I just love long division. I always get the wrong answer, but there is something just thrilling about the whole process." The perception of maths as 'methods to be learnt in order to get the right answer' is deep-rooted. The activities in this book are about much more than finding 'the right answer'. They often have many different possible solutions or no right or wrong answer at all. The point is for pupils to lose the fear of being wrong and learn by exploring, investigating, and thinking in depth.

'When will I ever need to know this in real life?'

Although many people won't use formal algebra or trigonometry once they leave school, there are some skills that maths develops which will be vital: noticing patterns, solving problems, checking solutions, trying different approaches, explaining reasons and thinking logically.

How to use this book

This book is designed to be practical and to be used flexibly. It will remain relevant to *any* curriculum or scheme of work as it is impossible to imagine calculation ever being dropped from a programme of study. Also, care has been taken to make sure the activities are relevant to pupils of any age and ability in KS2 (though could also be used in both KS1 and KS3) and contain modifications for how to differentiate them through challenge and support.

The activities are designed to be highly engaging and rich in mathematical content, and to prompt pupils to develop a deep conceptual understanding of calculation, rather than learning processes to follow without any real engagement. Some teachers will choose to dip into this book for lesson ideas and activities for groups of their pupils. Others may use the structure of the book to support longer-term planning.

The activities can be adapted for use in lessons in a number of ways:

- As **whole-class lessons** – The activities can be used with a whole class as part of a sequence of sessions teaching calculation. They contain notes for a variety of questions that can be used for a range of abilities, as well as notes for how to organise and engage the class.
- To support **differentiation** – the activities could be given to a group to support or enhance their learning within a lesson.
- **Supporting** specific pupils or groups – the activity notes could be given to a TA or used by a teacher for a guided group session, especially for assessment.
- For **assessment** – the activities can be used at the beginning or during a sequence about teaching to make a formative assessment to inform what the pupils' next steps are, or at the end of a sequence, to make a summative assessment of what they have learnt.

Types of activity

There are a range of different activities used throughout the book. Each activity is based around the following principles:

- Pupil engagement;
- Going beyond simply 'getting the right answer';
- Rich mathematical content.

The activities are categorised by how they can be used in school, though each activity can be adapted for a range of different purposes, both in and out of class.

Investigation: Each of these is built around a rich mathematical context. There are patterns and surprises for pupils to discover and explore. They will come up with their own theories and this will lead to further discussion, especially when the theories aren't correct. This will help build a sense of moving beyond 'one right answer'.

Outdoor learning: Pupils are often motivated by the outdoor environment, and going outside offers an excellent opportunity for pupils to develop a physical sense of number and calculation.

Quick activity: A quick idea for how to engage pupils and support or extend their learning. These ideas can be adapted for use in a minute or extended to be a whole-planned lesson.

Reflection: Use of time to pause and think about their own learning. This approach is sometimes termed 'metacognition'. These activities give the teachers and pupils the opportunity to notice how their understanding has developed.

Problem solving: These activities will tend towards an answer or a result. However, the 'answer' is not an end-point but should lead to deeper understanding, and more questions and puzzles to tackle.

Discussion points: A chance to consider interesting mathematical philosophical and paradoxical concepts in more depth.

This book can also be used to inform long and medium-term planning. It follows a progression of skills and understanding, and can be used to give a structure to teaching and learning over the course of a term or a school year.

Chapter summary

Chapter 1: This contains advice and activities to engage pupils in the patterns and flow of numbers and to notice how numbers apply to the world around them. It also contains simple ideas for enhancing the classroom environment, giving the pupils independence, challenge, and freeing up the teacher to support individual pupils.

Chapter 2: Develops some vital mental software to support their learning of calculation, for both more or less formal methods. Practising these skills will enhance the learning and understanding of all pupils, even those who seem to be proficient calculators already, as they strengthen the links between key concepts.

Chapter 3: Focuses on developing a deep conceptual understanding of the mechanics of calculation methods for the four operations, and on the links between them, building on the key concepts discussed in chapter 1.

Chapter 4: Extends pupils' understanding by giving them the opportunity to apply the skills learnt in chapters 1 and 2 to fraction and decimal numbers, and to a range of different contexts, involving deep mathematical thinking skills.

The structure can be used to build a progression of skills and understanding for pupils in the class, and likewise can be tailored to any programme of study your school may follow.

1
A Sense of Number

'If you want to build a ship, don't drum up people together, have them gather wood and set them tasks and work. But rather, teach them to long for the endless immensity of the sea.'

Antoine du Saint-Exupéry

Key concept

The activities in this chapter encourage pupils to see how numbers relate to them and to the world using the school environment, classroom resources, and pictures and diagrams. Pupils who have an intuition or 'a feel for' numbers will be able to make sense of the calculations they are asked to do, rather than blindly following a procedure. The aims are:

- To help teachers promote an interest in number.
- To attune pupils to patterns in number.
- Suggests strategies for a classroom rich in number.

Getting a feel for number

Pupils need to have an intuitive sense of the size of number, and in their early education they should have as many opportunities as possible to manipulate objects and groups of objects to develop their sense of the size of numbers, of comparing, of growing and shrinking, and of arranging and organising. The activities in this book are aimed primarily at pupils who are 7 or older, the majority of which will have had the chance to develop that 'size of number' sense through experience. However, there will be pupils of all ages who have not yet had enough experience to make full sense of the abstract notions of number and calculation, and ALL pupils enjoy investigating using objects to support their understanding.

Below are some examples of activities that can be used with very young pupils to build a sense of number, with older pupils who still need to experience number through objects, and with more able pupils whose understanding will be further enriched. It is well worth noting that 11 year olds enjoy 'playing' with building blocks as much as 4 year olds! The questions cover a range of difficulty and complexity and can be used to challenge all pupils, and make them think more deeply about calculation and different methods.

Building blocks

Take a box of building blocks and explore the following questions.

- How many do you think are in here?
- Do you think we have enough to make a tower that would be taller than you? How could we find out without building a tower that falls over? How many do you think we will need?
- Let's make a pyramid. How many do we need to put on the bottom row? What about the next row?
- What do we need to do if we want to make it taller?
- How tall a pyramid could I make if I had 100 blocks?
- Draw a shape on A3 paper. How could you use the blocks to estimate the area of this shape?
- How many blocks would fit in this crate if you stacked them very neatly? What if the box was twice as long?

Construction bricks

Bricks of the same size can be used to help children develop a sense of the size of numbers (cardinality). Explore the following using a set of joining construction bricks.

- Put the bricks in a row but leave a gap between two. What size brick would fit in this gap? How do you know?
- How many would we need to join together to get longer than a pencil, than your shoe, than my shoe?
- How many bricks would you need to go around the perimeter of your table?
- How many more bricks would I need to add to this pile to have enough to cover your exercise book?
- If this classroom was built out of these toy bricks, how many would you need?
- What different sized cubes could you make if you only had this type of brick?

Linking cubes

Linking cubes can be used to give a practical sense of number patterns and are a motivational context for exploring basic number concepts.

Number bond practice

Show pupils a row of blocks and carry out the following activities.

- Break a certain number off and hide them behind your back. Show the remaining ones. How many are hidden?
- Take one from behind your back and add it to the row. How many are hidden now?

Make a growing pattern (see below)

- Can you make the next one in my pattern?
- How many cubes would I need to take to make the 6th one in my pattern?
- Would 50 be enough to make the 12th one?

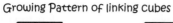

Growing Pattern of linking cubes

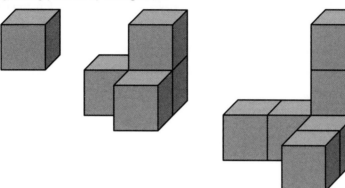

Make a cuboid (see below)

- What calculations could you use to work out how many cubes are used to make this?
- How many of the small cube faces are hidden from view?

Cuboid

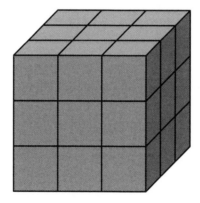

Toy cars

Toy cars provide the oppurtunity to model real life situations and help children develop the ability to unpick word problems.

- If you line up all these toy cars, how far will the line reach?
- Would this car roll more than a meter if you roll it down a ramp?

- Design a car park for these cars, so that you can fit 100 cars in without any of them being blocked.
- What proportion of these cars are silver?
- How many blue cars would we need to add so that there is a ratio of 3 red to 5 blue?

Toy people

Little figures are especially useful for introducing the basic concepts of grouping and sharing.

- How many shoes would you need to make for this group of people?
- Would fifty sweets be enough to give each person 5?
- What size groups can these people be arranged in so that no one is left without a group?
- If you wanted to share 47 horses between these people, so that each person got a prime number of horses, what different solutions are there?

Outdoor estimation

Pupils can become the mathematical 'apparatus' as they feature in the maths problem themselves.

- How many steps do you think it will take to walk all the way to the other side of the playground?
- Now, how many steps will it take to walk there and back?
- Estimate the number of branches on that tree. What about the number of leaves?
- Predict how long it will take to walk the perimeter of the field.
- Now predict how long it will take to walk the perimeter of the playground.
- Make an approximation of the area of the school grounds.
- Do you think 1000 is a good estimate for the number of bricks in the school?

Place value apparatus

Tens and ones apparatus can be used to begin to develop a more abstract understanding of number and of how the place value system we use relates to real life.

- I am going to show you a number on my fingers (e.g. 32 is 10 10 10 and 2). Can you make that number using the tens and ones equipment?
- What would I need to add to reach the next 10?
- Am I nearer to 20 or 50?
- Why is 27+95 tricky to show with this apparatus?
- Could you show how to find 61 – 34 using these?
- Using tens and units apparatus, demonstrate 365 divided by 7. What do you notice?
- How many different numbers can you represent if you have 2 hundreds, 7 tens and 3 units?

Playing cards

As well as offering the chance to play a range of games, using cards can be a very rich source of mathematical enquiry.

- What would be a good way to make sure we have got all of these cards?
- I have taken one of the cards out of the pack. How could you find which one is missing?
- Use the number cards as digit cards.
  - What is the second largest number I can make?
  - What is the nearest I can make to 3000 using some of these 5 cards as digits?
- Show a card pyramid:
  - How tall a pyramid could I make with 100 cards?
  - Estimate how long it would take.

Taking an interest in number

We want pupils to notice numbers and ponder them, both consciously and unconsciously, the way they might pick up a shell or a pebble on the beach, examine it, and then turn it over in their hands as they walk. Every pupil can become more attuned to mathematics, and their confidence will increase as a result simply of noticing.

Quick activity: number spotters

- This could be set as a quick weekend homework, or even as a lunchtime task.
- Give the pupils a number, 7 for example, and challenge them to notice how many different ways they can find that number. If they jot them down, like a bird-spotter, then they can return to class and see who has collected the rarest most interesting specimens.
- You can hope for a varied response: "There is a 7 on my TV remote", "There are seven doors in the upstairs of my house", "Seven is the third and fourth digit of my phone number", "My Gran lives next-door to number 77" and so on.
- You can vary the search by setting different groups of numbers to spot:

o Things that come in fours	o Numbers that end '99'	o Even multiples of 3
o Even numbers	o Consecutive numbers	o Quarters
o Square numbers	o Factors of 100	o Negative numbers
o Multiples of 5	o Decimals	o Prime numbers

- If you repeat it regularly, with a different focus each time, and share the results, then pupils will become more observant, more likely to notice numbers, and more inventive in their search.

Pupils will start to see numbers in two different ways: as numerals and digits on the one hand, and as ways of measuring and counting the world on the other. We want pupils to explore the properties of number. Going back to the beach, pupils take another look at their pebble, feel its smoothness, notice pock-marks or discolourations, notice how it is similar and different to the other pebbles around it, and start to consider how it came to be the way it is. They might, even, dash it apart to see what it is made of.

Discussion point: The meaning of calculate

The word 'calculate' comes from the Latin 'calculus', meaning stone or pebble. How could that have come about? What could possibly link the word for pebbles with the idea of adding, subtracting, multiplying or dividing?

A clue is that pebbles were used to keep count, tools to reckon with, in ancient times, a little like the beads on an abacus.

Reflection: Familiar numbers

Challenge pupils to think of as many ways as they can that these numbers are from 'real life'?

365	24	5
13	30	28
7	100	10
60	12	1000

Use these numbers in your teaching, as examples and as exercises for calculation practice – if pupils have worked out 24 x 7, then they will know how many hours in a week or how much you would need to pay Snow White's Dwarves for mining work at £24 a day. If they have worked out 60 x 60, then they know how many seconds in an hour. 11 x 20 tells you how many players play in 10 football matches. . .

Simpler questions for support
How old are you? What date is your birthday on? What number is your house? What is your lucky/favourite number? How many months until New Year?

Harder questions for greater challenge
How many days until your birthday? How many minutes until Christmas? How many times does the moon orbit the Earth in 10 years?

Patterns in number

Patterns are irresistible to humans – our brains are highly sophisticated pattern-spotting machines! As pupils see patterns emerging in calculations their brains will automatically start to work mathematically by:

- **Predicting** how the pattern will continue;
- Looking for **similarities** and **differences**;
- Looking for what **remains constant**, and what **changes**.

Their thinking will be greatly enhanced if they are supported in:

- **Checking** if their predictions were right;
- **Adjusting** their thinking where their predictions break-down;
- **Consider the reasons** for what causes the pattern.

Investigation: Beat the calculator

These calculations can be called **pyramid calculations** because of the way each layer grows. There are more detailed problem-solving activities which build on this task to generate real in-depth analysis of particular calculation methods later on in the book. Calculators on a computer will be most useful for this activity, as they can show more digits on the read-out than on a standard classroom calculator.

Ask pupils to work out the answers to the first two calculations in each pyramid using a calculator. Then pause – can they predict what the next answer will be in the sequence? The key question "What's the same, and what's different?" or "What stays the same and what changes?" can unlock pupils' thinking and reasoning skills. Insist they give a reason for why their prediction is more than just a guess or a hunch. Use calculators to check their predictions.

11 x 11	11 x 22	1001 x 274	101 x 32
111 x 111	111 x 222	1001001 x 274	10101 x 32
1111 x 1111	1111 x 2222	1001001001 x 274	1010101 x 32
. . .		. . .	. . .

Pupils can gain great confidence by seeing how their brain can become faster than a calculator. Once they have seen the pattern, they can work out answers to calculations that can't be displayed on a calculator read-out and they will be much faster than someone who has to type all the digits in.

This activity can be used with a whole class as a lesson starter, or as a small group investigation. It can be differentiated by asking different groups to work on different patterns or asking them to predict further along the pattern.

For people who are not confident in their own mathematical abilities, number can seem like a vast sea, immense and beyond understanding. Imagine if, to learn how to multiply, you had to just learn all the multiplications. Not just the times tables, but all of them: 17 x 39, 91 x 6, 17277 x 325, . . .

That there are patterns in numbers and in the way they behave is the only reason that we can do mathematics at all. Without pattern and regularity, we would have to sift through the endless immensity, one calculation at a time and learn them all off by heart.

Understanding that pattern is the basis of all calculation

For many pupils, that there are patterns in number and that we are allowed to use those patterns to help us, can be something of a revelation. To attune pupils to this fact, we can introduce a range of numbers with 'hooks' that fire the part of the brain that responds to pattern. Pupils should become familiar with these different numbers. They contain patterns that make the vast sea of numbers seem more comprehensible.

- Odds and evens
- Multiples of 10
- Multiples of 5
- Multiples of 11 and multiples of 9

How can you tell straight away which of these diagrams represent odd numbers?

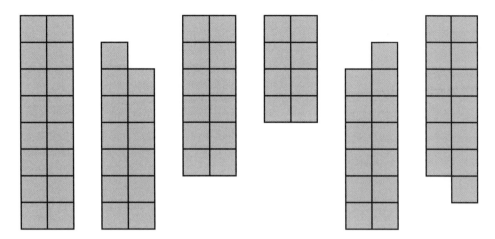

True or false?

It is important that pupil recognise the essential patterns but they can also gain a deeper understanding by taking them apart and putting them back together.

Give pupils the statements from the table below and ask if they think they are true or false. How can we find out?

- Guide pupils through trying some examples to see if they support the statement.
- Encourage pupils to realise that just trying one or two examples might not be enough because some of these statements might be true *and* false, depending on the numbers you choose.
- Discussion about why they are true or false will lift their understanding to another level. Having paper and coloured felt-tips, or objects such as bricks or counters can support real in-depth investigation and discussion.

Statements	Prompts for discussion
Even + Even = Even	Demonstrate how we can show even numbers by using objects or pictures with 2 rows.
Odd + Odd = Odd	Odd numbers can be shown as an even number and one extra.
Even − Odd = Even	Then, pupils can reason about whether the calculation leaves you with one left over at the end.

If you add two multiples of 10, you get a multiple of 10.	Begin by listing multiples of 10 and multiples of 5. Then, pick the numbers you need from each list, and examine the results.
If you add two multiples of 5, you get a multiple of 10.	Model discussion of the 'units digit'.
If you take away 5 from a multiple of 10, you get a multiple of 10.	Notice that some of these are sometimes true and sometimes false.
Multiples of 11 have repeated digits.	These are all sometimes true and sometimes false.
Multiples of 9 have repeated digits.	You will need to encourage pupils to look further, to extend the range of their examples. Can they think of any multiples of 11 larger than 100, for example. How can they find them out?
If you add the digits of a multiple of 9, they equal 9.	
If you add a multiple of 11 to a multiple of 9, you get a multiple of 10.	Which multiples of 11 are even? Which are odd? Could you predict whether 200 x 11 was even or odd?
Multiples of 11 are even.	
Multiples of 9 are odd.	

Classroom environment

There a many opportunities to make the most of the classroom environment and key moments of the school day. The activities given below will keep pupils engaged in number and pattern, and will support their understanding in maths lessons, boosting their confidence considerably. The cards below take hardly any time to prepare, cost almost nothing, and prompt deep mathematical thinking. Introduce a new one each week, to allow pupils to grasp each and to avoid over-whelming them.

Quick activity: Fact families

Rather than teaching facts such as times tables separately, teach them as families. The examples below can be written on separate cards and displayed in the classroom. They might even be spread out around the room so that pupils have to remember where to look for the different family of facts they need. Using this method, pupils will learn the relationships between the separate facts and be able to learn how to work out what they *don't* know by thinking about what they *do* know. For example, if pupils know 5 x 4 = 20, they can very quickly work out 6 x 4 and 4 x 4 by adding or subtracting 4.

The example oppposite is for the seven times table but it can be adapted for any times table using the same fact families. Leave them for all to see for the first week. Ask if pupils can spot how the facts in each family are 'related'. Then cover up different parts of each using post-it notes. If you cover up 28 and 42 on the third family, pupils will have to use the relationship they have spotted to figure out the unknown fact from 5 x 7 = 35.

When pupils have seen the patterns, and have gained confidence in a times table, have them create the next set of families for the next times table you want them to learn.

$1 \times 7 = 7$ $10 \times 7 = 70$ $100 \times 7 = 700$	$1 \times 7 = 7$ $10 \times 7 = 70$ $5 \times 7 = 35$	$4 \times 7 = 28$ $5 \times 7 = 35$ $6 \times 7 = 42$	$1 \times 7 = 7$ $2 \times 7 = 14$ $4 \times 7 = 28$ $8 \times 7 = 56$	$3 \times 7 = 21$ $6 \times 7 = 42$ $9 \times 7 = 63$	$7 \times 7 = 49$ $70 \times 7 = 490$ $700 \times 7 = 4900$
How could you work out 101×7? What about 1010×7?	How many 7s in 35? How many 7s in 350?	What is a quarter of 28? What is 20% of 35? How can you use this to work out $\frac{1}{6}$ of 42?	Is 100 an over- or an under-estimate for 16×7?	What do you notice when you add 3×7 to 6×7? (i.e. $21 + 42$)	How many division facts can you tell me from this family?

Questions to extend pupils' understanding are shown underneath each 'family'.

Even for pupils who are very proficient at their times tables these families can be used to prompt effective learning:

- Use these to learn the division facts as well: "How many 7s in 42?"
- Choose two families, and show how many different facts you can make by combining them.

The following questions can be used to support and challenge:

Support

- How many 7s in 70?
- Which is your favourite family? Why?
- Which families have 35 in? What do you notice?

Challenge

- How many square numbers are there in these families?
- What do you notice if you subtract two members of a family?
- Which families could you use to work out $4\frac{1}{2} \times 7$?
- What about 128×7?

Quick activity: Numbers of the week

This is incredibly easy to set up, to run, and to differentiate.

Laminate five different sheets of paper – they could be different colours or different shapes. At the start of each week, write a different number on each sheet. They could be linked (all even, all multiples of 10, all decimals) or random. These numbers can then be used for a range of questions over the week and for a regular starter on a Monday. After you have modelled this for a couple of weeks to the class, you can just display these questions on a Monday morning and the children will settle to their work. The questions get increasingly challenging and they also revise key skills.

- Write the numbers in order, from smallest to largest?
- Put all the numbers on an empty number line. Try to be as precise as you can.
- Write a calculation for the class to try using these numbers.
- What do I have to add to each number to make 20/100/1000?
- Double/halve each number.
- Multiply each number by 10/100/1000. Divide each number by 10.
- Find the sum of three different pairs.
- What is the total of all the numbers?
- Add 9/99/999 to each number.
- What is the difference between the largest and the smallest?
- Draw two different arrays for green/pentagon.
- Find the product of blue and yellow/triangle and square?
- Describe an efficient method for finding the total of them all.
- Find (blue x 10) – blue.
- Which number has the most factors?
- Which number is closest to a square number?
- Use the numbers to make a fraction equivalent to a half, a quarter, a third. What's the closest you can get to each?
- Use the numbers to write a division that has the smallest possible remainder/gives a recurring decimal.
- Use all four operations and brackets, how close can you get to 100? 99? 500?. . .

You can also use them to begin introducing algebraic notation.

- $b + y = ?$
- $b + ? = r - 1$
- $? \times g = y - ?$

Quick activity: Lunch register

Ask the pupils to respond with a different type of number or calculation depending on what lunch they're having, for example:

School dinner = Even number	Packed lunch = Odd number
School dinner = Multiple of 10	Packed lunch = Not a multiple of 10

You can challenge more able pupils to give you a calculation that results in the appropriate kind of number, and insist, for example, that their calculation includes an addition and a multiplication.

Quick activity: Target envelopes

It is important for a pupil to know what they need to practise in order to get better. Give the pupils a large envelope each, to keep in their trays. In the envelope they can keep small target cards. Here are some suggested cards:

- Times table/number bond flash cards: write the calculation on one side, and the answer on the reverse. They can then practise with a partner at any time.

- Mistake cards: a range of written calculations with a mistake hidden in them. Pupils have to find the mistake, and describe it to a partner. These can pick out key mistakes that the pupil often makes (65 + 45 = 100, for example), and serve as regular reminders.

- Written method examples: this can be a perfect example on one side, and then a range of numbers to practise with on the reverse.

- Vocabulary and sentence starters: key vocabulary and sentence fragments that pupils can join together to write sentences about the properties of number for example.

Quick activity: Password

Put a code on the door, and demand a password from the pupils before they enter or exit. *It's important to make sure that this is not threatening*, and also that the pupils want to come into the classroom in the first place! It could be as simple as a laminated sheet of card with two numbers written with a gap between. You can then easily differentiate the question you ask pupils: Tell me a number in the gap. . . for example tell me any number between these two, tell me a square number between them, tell me a prime number between these two, tell me a multiple of 5 between these two, tell me a decimal number. . .

Problem solving: The dog ate my homework

This is really useful for "I've finished, what shall I do now?" Turn up to class with a story of woe:

"My son/niece came to me in floods of tears. They spent ages on their maths homework at the weekend, but then a terrible thing happened: their dog ACTUALLY ate their homework. All that was left was this."

(Hold up a scrap of paper, with '= 24' just visible.)

"We know the answer, but you have to show your working to get the mark, and my son/niece can't remember the question that was asked. It's due on Friday. Can you help? Can you think of as many possible questions as you can with the answer 24? Surely, if we think of enough possibilities, we will come up with the right question."

Display the scrap on a noticeboard in the classroom. In any free moments, pupils could think of possible questions with the correct answer, check their working, and then write them on a note to be pinned up with the answer. Encourage pupils to be inventive, and vary the challenge by 'remembering' certain details throughout the day.

- I think it had an addition and a subtraction.
- I think it was a word problem about eggs/ about the cost of going to the cinema. . .
- I think there were decimals or fractions involved.
- I think it has three steps to solve it.
- We know that one part of it was about dividing by 100.

You can also target certain pupils:

- Jenna – I think it might have been about percentages.
- Bilal – we think it included two different square numbers.
- Sam – I am sure it was something about number bonds to 100.

For the next week, you can go through the same process, but with an even more outlandish story:

- All that was left was this corner of work, after the rocket boosters fired and the aliens took off in their ship.
- And so we managed to save the princess, but the horse trampled the homework into the mud.
- The wizard blasted us with a spell, but the homework protected us. Unfortunately, it was vaporised except for this tiny scrap.

Some groups of pupils might enjoy making up the next story for the next week, as a fun piece of adventure writing.

Quick activity: PE warm-up

While warming up for PE, pupils could march while counting in twos or tens, or decimals, or do a call and response drill.

Call and response for commutativity:
Leader: "Two times four is. . ."
Response "Four times two."
Leader: "Ten add thirty is. . ."
Response "Thirty add ten is. . ."

When setting a number of star jumps, give it as a calculation: "Now do 3 x 2 star jumps." "Do the number of squat thrusts you have to add to 13 to get 20."

Mathematical stamina and esteem – maths as an emotional activity

Celebrating mistakes

Pupils need to feel that it is fine to make mistakes, to not know the answer, to feel anxiety. We need to give them the skills and resilience to be able to face their challenges. The healthiest classes are the ones in which people are willing to take the risk of being wrong.

Celebrate mistakes for the following reasons:

- Someone has been willing to face a challenge.
- It is an opportunity to learn something new.
- It will help other people who would have made the mistake as well.
- It might set us down a new path, a way of thinking that no one has ever tried before.

Likewise, celebrate your own mistakes as a teacher and admit to not being sure sometimes.

- "I don't know the answer to that, but I can think of a way to begin finding out. How would you begin?"
- "I am not sure. Shall we try. . ."
- "I wonder why I made that mistake? How can I make sure I keep a look out for it next time?"

There are some key strategies that are easy to implement:

Beginning questions

- Tell me about this calculation.
- What do you notice about this calculation?
- What might someone find tricky about this?
- How could I begin?

Estimation techniques

- Tell me an answer that's too large. And one that's too small. So it's somewhere between . . . and . . .
- I thought the answer might be about 200. Is that a reasonable estimate?
- I guess the units digit will be a zero because. . . What do you think?

How many solutions?

- Can you find more than one solution to. . . ? + ? + ? = 15
- Are there more than 10 different ways of. . . odd + odd + even + even = 20
- Find an easy and a complicated solution to. . . ? − 10 = 10 x ?

Multiple choice

Multiple choice questions can be very useful as pupils can reason their way to an answer even if they're not sure how to go through the whole process themselves. This encourages them to look at the structure of the calculation, rather than just churning out the correct answer.

For example:

- What is 32 x 20: a) 52 b) 320 c) 640 d) 64
- What is 53 + 99 a) 153 b) 154 c) 46 d) 152

Notice how in each there are good reasons for being able to eliminate each incorrect answer. For 32 x 20, it can't be 320 because that is 32 x 10, it can't be 64 because that is double 32. 52 looks far too small (what mistake has been made for that?). . .

Making deliberate mistakes

Spotting the error is vital for being able to self-check. There is little point in a pupil doing corrections if they are unable to see where or why calculations have gone wrong. As a plenary to review a new method for calculation, put up three examples that each contain an error. Pupils enjoy spotting errors and it helps to highlight common mistakes. You can also set up a whole task so that pupils have to aim for the incorrect answer. Many reluctant pupils will enjoy this as it seems to release some of the pressure. However, they need to look at the structure of the problem and make mathematical decisions.

Use all these digits once to make all the answers to these wrong. How can you be sure?

1, 2, 3, 4, 5, 0

?? is a multiple of 10

?? is an even number

? + ? is an odd number

A very useful way to model mistakes is to use a character. They can also model the kind of language used to give reasons for your thinking, which is a vital skill that is difficult to teach directly.

For example:

- My cat Jeoffrey thinks that 20 x 7 is 80 because he knows that 10 x 7 is 70, but 20 is 10 more so he has added 10 to 70.
- My dog Suzie thinks that 20 x 7 is 114 because 20 is double 10, and 14 is double 7, and the answer has to be more than 100 because 10 x 7 is nearly 100.

Ask pupils if they can spot any good thinking from Jeoffrey or Suzie. Praise their thinking, and the way they have thought about the numbers.

- Can anyone spot any mistakes they might have made?
- What doesn't Jeoffrey know yet that we can help him with?
- Without just telling them the right answer, how could we help pupils improve their understanding?

2
Mastery of Three Key Models

Key concept

The mantra 'All maths is mental maths' is powerful. Written methods for calculation are very useful but pupils will not retain them or be able to apply them if they do not have an understanding of how they work. In this chapter, we look at developing mental software for how numbers and calculations behave—pictures that pupils can store and manipulate in their brains and carry with them wherever they go. The aim is:

- To develop vital 'mental software' using:
  - 100 squares
  - Number lines
  - Arrays

The three models chosen are versatile and display key concepts very clearly. However, it is important to be aware that they are only useful if pupils understand how they work and can see how they relate to the numbers and the calculations themselves.

Moving from using objects to mental strategies

If pupils can count objects, then they can solve most calculations. For example, if you needed to solve 74 – 59, you could count out 74 pebbles, then take away one at a time until you have counted 59 away, then begin counting again with the pile you have left. This is a perfectly valid way of solving the problem, and will give the answer 15, so long as the counting is accurate. However, it is time-consuming, and it is prone to error. BUT it is a starting point – so every child should feel that they can calculate in line with their ability to count.

Reflection: Pebble calculations for the Stone Age

Demonstrate pebble calculation for 13 + 15:

Count out 13, then add one at a time counting until you have added 15, then count the whole group. You could do this in silence and then ask the children if they can suggest what you were trying to work out; can they write it as a calculation? Ask pupils to explain your method back to you or to a partner.

Did they notice any things you were doing to make sure you were accurate?

Did they notice you keeping certain piles separate?

Did they notice you counting each individual pebble carefully and knowing when to go back to zero before counting again?

Could it have been done in another way? (Perhaps count out a pile of 13, then a pile of 15, and then combine the piles and count them all).

Now challenge pupils to create a 'pebble method' for: 28 + 15, 28 – 15, 5 x 5 and 32 ÷ 8. Challenge them to create a method that requires the person only to know how to count. Many children will be able to calculate the answers without using the pebbles but explain that the focus is on the method and the link between counting and calculating. Afterwards, challenge pupils to think of ways to make the process more efficient, quicker, and less prone to error. They might suggest counting in twos, or groups of 10, or using rows and columns.

To solve pebble calculations, pupils need to know what add 'means', how subtraction relates to taking away, how division can be solved by grouping or sharing, and so on. What it does is focus in on the behaviour of the calculations, rather than the numbers involved. It is well worth returning to this regularly as it will give you an insight into the pupils' understanding rather than simply their skill with number.

We can think of calculation methods as ways of making the process more efficient, harnessing place value and pattern to simplify and speed-up our thinking. The images used in the next part: 100 squares, number lines and arrays are powerful because they enable pupils to visualise the calculations in a way that relates to the numbers that we use to count. They are also FLEXIBLE – we can adapt the images to our needs and the needs of a calculation. The aim is for pupils to be able to build enough familiarity and understanding that they can internalise the images and have a flexible mental software to apply to calculations.

Harnessing the power of 100 squares

100 squares are powerful because they are so rich in pattern. This makes them engaging and memorable – with a little practice pupils can visualise a 100 square and use its structure to support their written mental calculations.

There are two aims:

1 Pupils learn to 'see' a 100 square in their mind.
2 Pupils use 100 squares to discover rich patterns that exist in numbers.

These two aims go hand-in-hand and the activities in this chapter will build on each.

What's the same and what's different?

Looking for **similarities** and **differences** is one of the most important mathematical skills. There are two common variations of the 100 square, shown opposite. Ask pupils to spot similarities and differences between them. Insist that they look deeply into the structure and mine them for as much information as they can. The rows and columns have been highlighted to draw out some of the patterns. There are subtle differences – challenge pupils to look as closely as possible.

0	1	2	3	4	5	6	7	8	9
10	11	12	13	14	15	16	17	18	19
20	21	22	23	24	25	26	27	28	29
30	31	32	33	34	35	36	37	38	39
40	41	42	43	44	45	46	47	48	49
50	51	52	53	54	55	56	57	58	59
60	61	62	63	64	65	66	67	68	69
70	71	72	73	74	75	76	77	78	79
80	81	82	83	84	85	86	87	88	89
90	91	92	93	94	95	96	97	98	99

1	2	3	4	5	6	7	8	9	10
11	12	13	14	15	16	17	18	19	20
21	22	23	24	25	26	27	28	29	30
31	32	33	34	35	36	37	38	39	40
41	42	43	44	45	46	47	48	49	50
51	52	53	54	55	56	57	58	59	60
61	62	63	64	65	66	67	68	69	70
71	72	73	74	75	76	77	78	79	80
81	82	83	84	85	86	87	88	89	90
91	92	93	94	95	96	97	98	99	100

Pupils will need to learn vocabulary for rows, columns and digits. Model the language as follows:

- The row that begins with the number 30.
- The column where the unit digits are all 7.
- The tens digit increases by 1 when you move down a row.

Discussion point: Teaching specific vocabulary (not just because it sounds better!)

When discussing their findings, pupils will often begin to use vague terms and confused half-sentences. For example: "It goes up in ones every time"; "That line is all the same for the last number but not the tens"; "It always goes that way and only one number changes".

The vagueness and confusion can have two negative impacts:

1 Frustration – pupils can't say what they know.
2 Error – misconceptions can be caused where the language is not precise.

BUT – it is important that pupils understand why using certain vocabulary can make their lives easier.

Rather than just correcting mistakes there are a number of ways to help pupils gain confidence:

Rehearse: at the beginning of a session, use and repeat the language as a class as if learning lines for a play.
Sympathise: when pupils are struggling to explain an idea, encourage them by noticing what a tricky concept they are trying to communicate and how difficult it can be to express.
Reflect: model back to pupils what they have said and alter it to use more 'correct' vocabulary.

Some common misuses linked with 100 squares are below:

Misuse	Example	Why the correct terminology is useful
'Number' used instead of 'digit'.	Because the last number is a 5.	Being able to talk about digits within a number, for example the digit 5 in the number 435, allows pupils to investigate and share many properties of number: odds/evens, multiples of 5 and 10, rounding, decimals, and many more.
'Sum' used for any calculation.	I did my sum and I found out that 99 – 32 is 67.	Sum is used specifically for addition. Pupils will be asked "Find the sum of 56 and 55".
'Line' used instead of 'row' or 'column'.	That line has all threes in it.	In 100 squares, it is vital to be able to distinguish between rows and columns, as the flow of numbers is different for each.

Reflection: 100 squares

Which 100 square do you think is most useful? Which do you prefer? Which would you choose to help with calculations? Would you change anything about either of them?

Pattern

Here are some of questions that prompt pupils to investigate the structure of hundred squares:

- Choose one column – look at the tens digits. What do you notice?
- Choose one row – what do you notice about the tens digits and the units digits?
- What happens to the digits if you move diagonally? What about if you move diagonally the other way? Why do you think it happens?
- Can you think what would be in the next row? What about the row after that?
- How many '3's are there? How many '9's?
- Which digit appears least/most often?
- I choose a number and add 5 to it. I end up here. Where did I start?
- I add 5 to a number in this row and end up in the next row. How many numbers could I have started on?
- I choose a number and add 9 to it. I end up on the same row. What number could I have chosen to start from?
- I start on the number 33. I take away more than 10 from it. I end up on the same column. What could I have taken away?

- I start on an odd number. I add a number less than 10 to it and I end up on an even number. What can you tell me about what I added?

- I choose a number, I double it and I end up in the row that begins with 80. What numbers could I have started with? Can you find them all?

- I choose a number. I double it and take away 10. I end up on the last row. What number could I have started with?

These questions will provide a good basis for your assessment of how well pupils can see how the structure of a 100 square relates to number and place value. Encourage pupils to explain their thinking in words, using props and also with diagrams.

Counting and moving

1	2	3	4	5	6	7	8	9	10
11	12	13	14	15	16	17	18	19	20
21	22	23	24	25	26	27	28	29	30
31	32	33	34	35	36	37	38	39	40
41	42	43	44	45	46	47	48	49	50
51	52	53	54	55	56	57	58	59	60
61	62	63	64	65	66	67	68	69	70
71	72	73	74	75	76	77	78	79	80
81	82	83	84	85	86	87	88	89	90
91	92	93	94	95	96	97	98	99	100

Having a physical and visual experience of number will enrich all pupils' understanding but is especially vital for those who are not so confident. 100 squares make an excellent scaffold for pupils to support their initial understanding. They can help unlock the patterns in sequences of numbers they have learnt early on.

Use a 100 square to highlight the 5s, 10s and 2s which pupils will be used to chanting. Have pupils follow the pattern with their finger, so that the rhythm of the chant becomes linked with the rhythm of movement. The pattern of counting in 5s becomes like a game of tennis when followed with the finger (5, 10, 15, 20, . . .). The pattern for counting in 2s is more like a typewriter (going from left to right in rows), whereas counting in 10s might be described as a lift. Allow the pupils to name the different patterns themselves.

Investigation: Tubes and stairs

Give pupils a number of 100 squares each and ask them to colour or shade all the even numbers. Model how they can begin by working across the rows. Allow pupils to carry on themselves. Very soon they will notice that it is quicker just to colour in the columns, as all the multiples of two are in regular columns. Now, model shading multiples of 3 in the first row of a fresh 100 square. Will this one go in columns as well? Allow pupils to continue the pattern. After a while, most will notice that the pattern is diagonal. Now, say to the class that one of these patterns is called 'Tubes' and one 'Staircases'. Which do pupils think is which? Why?

Independent task

Prediction activity: What other multiples or counting patterns might produce 'tubes' or 'staircases'? Now, pupils can use the rest of their 100 squares to hunt for more tubes and staircases by shading in different multiples. While pupils are working independently they will find new patterns that look like broken staircases. Allowing pupils to think of names for these will encourage them to use their imaginations and to become more engaged in the task. You can focus on pupils who struggle to recreate patterns accurately and at the same time display the following probing questions to encourage pupils to analyse their findings in greater detail:

- Which numbers are shaded in both the 3 and the 4 times tables?
- How many are shaded in each row? Are there always the same number shaded in each row?
- How many different patterns have the number 24 shaded? What about the number 99?
- What happens if you shade the multiples of 5 and the multiples of 6 on the same square?
- Are there more tubes, or more staircases?
- Do all staircases go from top left to bottom right?
- What would the patterns look like if you had a 100 square with a different starting number?

Encourage pupils to sort their 100 squares into groups and then compare them. What are the similarities and differences between all the 'staircases'? What about the 'tubes'? By comparing like this you can draw out discussions about how the patterns relate to each other. For a plenary look at the pattern of multiples of 11. This can draw out some of the reasons behind the patterns. Because 11 is 1 more than 10, the shading moves one column to the right for every row it moves down. This relationship between the shaded multiples and the number 10 is the key to understanding the mathematics behind this activity.

This activity is an excellent assessment opportunity. Pupils who do not see the regularity, or whose shading is incorrect will need to practise this a lot, and to develop their visual awareness through many pattern activities. Without developing this skill, they will continue to struggle in a wide variety of mathematical tasks.

Using versus learning

Visual and physical representations can help support pupils when they work with number. However, we need to teach pupils to use them as a springboard rather than as a crutch. Pupils need to gain understanding from using 100 squares rather than simply using them to get an answer. There is a difference between using a 100 square to add 10 and using it to learn *how* to add 10. If a pupil is told that you find '10 more' by looking for the number directly below, then they may gain very little understanding. If, however, they link adding 10 with how the units digit remains the same and the tens digit increases by 1, and also with how adding 1 ten times moves you across a row and requires a jump to the next row, then they will understand more fully and for longer, perhaps forever!

The 100 square is so rich in structure and pattern that nearly all pupils can learn to 'see' one in their mind quite quickly. That is not to say they should not have access to actual 100 squares nor be encouraged to use them in order to discover patterns and generalities.

Problem solving: Fill in the blanks

Regular starters involving figuring out the blanks in 100 squares can engage pupils' brains in number patterns ready for a lesson on number.

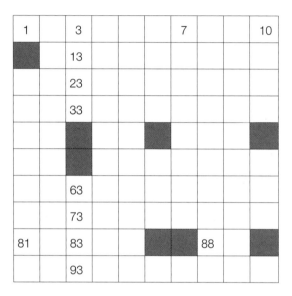

Here are some questions to open up all pupils' thinking:

- Which is the easiest shaded number to work out?
- Which takes the longest to work out?
- How can you quickly tell 91 is not one of the shaded numbers?
- How many steps does it take to work out whether 56 is shaded?
- How many different ways can you work out this shaded number? [point at any one]
- Where would you place a shaded square to make it as tricky as possible?
- How can you count all the multiples of 5 that are shaded?
- How many shaded squares are next to a square number?

Notice how these questions require more consideration than just finding the answers. By thinking about these questions pupils will develop their number awareness but also their awareness of how to solve problems. Even pupils for whom the number work is not challenging will gain understanding by thinking about these questions.

Quick sketches

Using spatial jottings can help pupils match written calculations with the effect of the calculation on the number. Encourage pupils to write the steps in their thinking according to the positions on a 100 square.

Quick sketches of parts of a 100 square to support addition. Pupils can draw these as they're working and start to visualise them after building confidence.

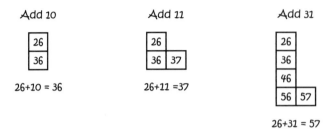

Add 10

| 26 |
| 36 |

26+10 = 36

Add 11

| 26 | |
| 36 | 37 |

26+11 =37

Add 31

26	
36	
46	
56	57

26+31 = 57

Reflection: Mental calculations

You can ask the same mental calculation in different ways. Which, if any, is more challenging? Here are some different ways of asking pupils to think about the same calculation:

- What is 45 + 32?
- What number is three rows below and 2 to the right of 45?
- Where is the number that is 32 more than 45?

How many different ways can you ask a question that is equivalent to the calculation 26 + 41?

Problem solving: X marks the spot (1)

This could be displayed as a picture on the board in class or made out of a piece of card. Many interesting questions can be asked, especially if it is made out of card, as it can be given to the pupils to explore and it can be rotated to provide further questions.

- How many numbers can you think of that x definitely is not?
- Give me 3 possible options for what x could be.
- Where would 11 more than x be?
- Do you think x is odd or even? Why?
- If I told you that x was a multiple of 5 would you agree? What about a multiple of 9?
- What could x be a multiple of?

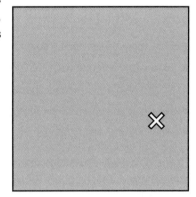

You can then make many simple variations of this problem by rotating the square so that x appears in a new position.

100 square variations

Pupils will truly master 100 squares once they have taken them apart and then put them back together again to see how they work. There are a number of very simple variations:

- Different starting numbers: What if the square began with 25?
- Different flow of numbers: What is the numbers flowed from right to left? Or from top to bottom?
- Different number of columns: If the 100 square had 11 columns, how would you add 10?

Once pupils are comfortable with the standard 100 square, then they can go through the same tasks but under different variations. For example, the 'x marks the spot' activity opposite can be enriched very simply by asking what x would be if the first number was 50 or 12 or 1000.

Outdoor learning: Jack and the hundred square

Setting up and class organisation

Take the class out to the playground, the field, or a courtyard or the school hall – anywhere that is large enough for the children to imagine they are *in* a 100 square. Agree with the pupils the boundaries of the giant 100 square and where the starting number is. Ask the children to go and stand in a space in the square and then decide what number they are on.

Questions everyone can attempt at the same time:

- Point to the person nearest to you. What number do you think they are on?
- Move to the number 1 more than you? Did any of you have to move far?
- Now move to 10 more than where you are. Point to where you started. What calculation would you have to do to get close to where you started?
- Point to the nearest multiple of 5.
- Move to the number you would have to add to yours to make 100.

Questions for individuals:

- Move to the nearest square number.
- Swap with so-and-so. What calculation would get you back to where you were?
- Move to the number half-way between you and 100.

Follow-up

Have everyone stand in the square. Take photos of the square from different angles. When back in class, display the photo and ask pupils to estimate the numbers for everyone else. What clues will they need to use? Which photo is most useful? You can even set calculations for the class to try out using pupils names as a kind of algebra:

Ross + Natasha = ?

Sara – ? = Ahmed

Varying the number of columns is a very good way of getting pupils to 'think again' and to understand the reason behind the patterns on a 100 square. The reason why adding 10 is so satisfying on a 100 square is precisely because there are 10 numbers in every row. The reason why the units digits change so pleasingly is because the number of columns matches the cycle of our counting numbers (technically this is called 'base 10'). And, digging a little deeper, the reason why the multiples of 9 and 11 make diagonal patterns is because 9 and 11 are just one more or less than 10.

columns. The pupils' challenge is to use scissors to convert their 10-column square into a 9-column number grid but before they cut or slice a thing, they have to make two predictions:

1 How many cuts will they have to make?
2 What will happen to the patterns of the multiples they shaded?

Before the pupils are allowed to use any scissors they should discuss their methods with a partner. However, for this activity it is best to allow the pupils opportunities to make mistakes and need to begin again. A certain amount of trial and error will help pupils understand this task more deeply than if they just followed a set of instructions.

There are a few errors or inefficiencies that are likely to happen:

• They cut every number individually so that they have to glue 100 tiny squares back down.
• They cut the right-most column from the 100 square and think they have completed the task.
• They stick the numbers with irregular gaps and so lose the columns structure.

Share these mistakes as useful examples of trial and error and draw out what has gone wrong. An atmosphere of 'helpful mistakes' is a sign of a very healthy classroom.

To differentiate:

1 Often pupils who do not consider themselves the 'best in the class' are more successful at this task than the 'high-flyers'. It is a good opportunity for them to lead the way.
2 Early finishers can investigate how you add or subtract 10 on the new number square.
3 Some may be interested in creating 11-column hundred squares and comparing the patterns of multiples.

Next steps
Useful plenary questions:

1 Have we created 100 squares or do we need a different name?
2 What did pupils decide to do with the 'left-over' number?
3 What patterns do you notice?
4 How can you use the 100 square to support addition and subtraction?
5 Which patterns are the same and which different if you compare the 100 squares?
6 Why are the multiple patterns different?
7 What pattern would multiples of 9 make on an 8-column square?

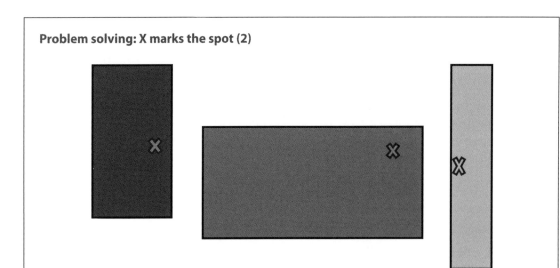
Harnessing the power of number lines

Number lines are powerful because they are so flexible, and so representative of the flow of numbers. Because of this they are more powerful than 100 squares but also more complex to learn and understand fully.

WARNING! – It is easy to over estimate how well a pupil understands the number line. Pupils can learn to follow certain steps to produce an answer to a certain type of calculation but then be stumped when posed a slightly different challenge.

Discussion point: Number lines everywhere

Where do we see number lines? They are not just for maths lessons and there are practical applications everywhere. Challenge pupils to be on the lookout for them. Below are some suggestions for where to begin looking.

- Measuring jugs
- Maps
- Tape measures and rulers
- Axes on graphs

- Speedometers on a dashboard
- Timelines

What makes a number line a number line? What can be measured with a number line? Are there things that can't be measured with a number line? You could set this as a homework for pupils: How many different number lines can they find over the weekend.

Hidden assumptions and misconceptions

Number lines are deceptive. There is a real difference between being shown how to use a number line and understanding how they work. If pupils can master the mechanics of a number line then they will have access to an incredibly useful tool for manipulating number especially for addition and subtraction. There are some 'hidden' aspects of how we tend to use number lines that can be very useful to consider when teaching and should be discussed directly with pupils.

Discussion point: Left to right

There is a largely unspoken rule that numbers increase from left to right on a number line. Does it need to be that way? Are there number lines that don't work like that? In fact, there are many number lines that are not even horizontal. Think of a scale on a measuring jug or on a thermometer or the y-axis on a coordinate grid. What do you notice about these number lines and the direction for numbers increasing? [They nearly always increase as you move 'up' the vertical number line.]

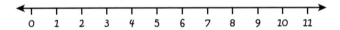

Following the left-right convention is helpful to most pupils, as they can then 'travel' to the right and know that the numbers will increase and be confident that when moving to the left the numbers will decrease.

When pupils first experience number lines, they tend to have the numbers written on them and are often used to support counting on and counting back.

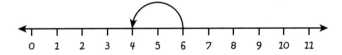

As pupils gain confidence they will begin to see number lines that do not have all the numbers written on them. These are sometimes referred to as 'blank' number lines. The increased understanding this requires should be taken into consideration. Pupils who can use blank number lines need to have the sense that *they are in charge* of the numbers and that they can choose which numbers to represent depending on the problem. This shift in thinking is vital and requires practice.

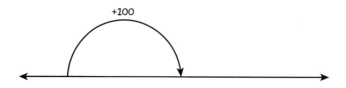

Reflection: Number lines

What are the stages of understanding that pupils go through in coming to terms with a number line? Consider what pupils need to understand to be able to interpret the number lines below. You could show a range of these number lines to pupils and ask them the very simple and important question: "What are the similarities and differences between these?" They will surprise you with the depth of their insight.

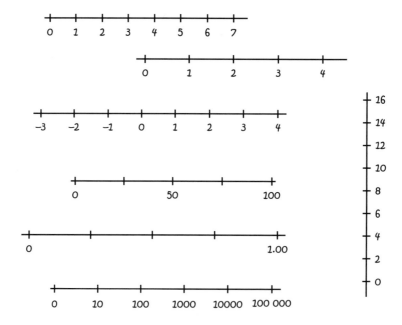

Drawing number lines is a very useful skill for pupils to develop. Encourage pupils to develop the skill of drawing them quickly and clearly rather than providing printed lines. This way pupils develop their flexibility of approach.

Ordinality and cardinality

The words 'ordinality' and 'cardinality' seem daunting, but they highlight two important ideas that can be described very simply, and pupils will be able to learn to use them very quickly.

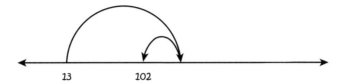

This is an ordinal number line because the numbers are in order, but the gaps between them are not to scale. Ordinality is how number lines are often talked about. It is to do with the order of the numbers (which can be a good way to remember the vocabulary). When asked "Where is fourteen?" pupils will most likely point to the number 14 as it is written on the line, the one between 13 and 15. Most people understand number lines in that way and talk about the numbers on them in that way: "Find 2 more than 14" means "look for the number 2 to the right of 14" and so on.

Cardinality is about how 'big' numbers are. What is the size of the number 14? This can be understood by imagining using a tape measure. At one point it will say 14cm. So the written number 14 is at that one point but 14cm is actually the distance from 0 to 14. 14cm is *that big*. The distinction between thinking in an ordinal way and in a cardinal way can help make sense of calculations. Also, pupils with an intuitive sense of the size of numbers will be more able to understand their calculations and make sense of them. They are also the pupils who will be better able to spot their own mistakes.

Outdoor learning: Ordinal and cardinal solar system

Our Solar System

My Very Easy Method Just Speeds Up Naming (Planets)

Since Pluto was declassified, the mnemonic above has become slightly less helpful but pupils will still learn the order of the planets. Show pupils a picture of the solar system, with the planets in order but not to scale. This represents an ordinal number line. We can also create a cardinal version using cones in an empty playground or outside space.

The distance of the planet Earth from the Sun is called 1 Astronomical Unit (1 AU). Pupils can put one cone down where they stand and then take 1 pace and put a second cone down. The first represents the Sun, the second represents Earth. Then pupils can use the table below to pace out a cardinal version of the solar system using 1 pace for 1 AU. When they have finished, the cones will be in order but they will also show the size of the distances between the planets.

Planet	Mercury	Venus	Earth	Mars	Jupiter	Saturn	Uranus	Neptune
Distance from Sun (approx..)	½ AU	¾ AU	1 AU	1½ AU	5 AU	9½ AU	19 AU	30 AU

Pupils can all explore the mechanics of number lines in the same way that they explore tape measures to see how they work. Rather than simply *using* number lines, pupils will learn to *master* them.

Using versus learning

There is a subtle but important difference between using number lines to to add and learning to add by using them. If you give pupils the number line pictured below numbered from 0 to 20 and show them how to count on and count back, then they will be able to use it to find out the answer to any addition or subtraction within that range.

However, a pupil may learn nothing by doing so except how to count on and back along the line. The pupil will not have developed any understanding until they have begun to internalise and visualise the idea. There are some simple ways to develop understanding.

- **Predict**: before counting on or back ask pupils to predict where they will land. They could predict a region rather than an exact answer.
- **Estimate**: ask if they think their answer will be above or below a certain number, say 10. Ask for reasons why they think it will be above or below?
- **Compare**: ask pupils to demonstrate how to perform the same calculation on a number line and on a hundred square. What is the same and what is different about the process? Some pupils may even be surprised that they produce the same answer.
- **Analyse**: make deliberate mistakes and have children look out for the error. Errors can include: counting in the wrong direction, inaccurate counting, missing jumps, . . .
- **Criticise:** ask pupils to think of ways to improve or speed up the process. Could they count in twos? What about a jump of 10 if they are subtracting 9?
- **Extend**: if we know $15 + 3 = 18$, what other facts could we work out? What about $15 + 4$? What about $18 - 3$? What about $115 + 3$? What about $? + 3 = 318$. . .

All of the above can be used with pupils who are already proficient in order to deepen their understanding. For example, you could ask a pupil to draw two number lines, one that shows an efficient way to add 99 to 27 and one that shows a very time consuming way. Very confident pupils will continue to benefit from deepening their understanding of number lines and how they relate to operations of addition and subtraction. When they come to calculate with positive and negative numbers and to use decimals and later to learn about significant figures and irrational numbers, or even calculus, the number line will be an incredibly powerful mental image.

Quick activity: Inventing scales

It can be illuminating to use mathematical ideas in non-mathematical ways. Below is a scale showing degrees of happiness:

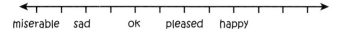

Ask if the pupils can fill in any other parts of the scale? Where would 'over joyed' go? What about 'quite happy'? Can they think of anything that would go to the left of 'miserable'? This kind of scaling is useful as well as imaginative. Pupils could draw an arrow on a scale to show how well they have understood a lesson or how confident they feel about division or how they predict they will perform in a football match. This kind of thinking can help pupils see how number lines work irrespective of numbers used. It can also be used to give an insight into a person's inner experience: if you had to rate your pain/fear on a scale of 1–10. . .

They could invent their own scales for:

   Comparing the fun levels of stalls/rides at a funfair (mega boring, yawn, not bad, . . .)
   Ordering the dangerousness of activities (lethal, extremely hazardous, perilous, safe, . . .)

A physical sense of number lines

Some pupils will understand number lines visually but some may need to build a physical sense of them as well in order to make sense of their structure. There are a number of opportunities to do this around the school and pupils should practise moving around lines and also getting a sense of how big numbers are. The school will almost certainly have lines marked out in the hall or on the playground and field. These can be used as big number lines for the pupils to walk, run and hop along, with cards to mark the numbers if needed. There are also some opportunities to develop a finer sense of number.

Outdoor learning: Ball of wool

Give pupils in pairs a ball of wool, a recording sheet and some pieces of paper with tape. They should choose one end of the wool as the start and go around the school measuring the length of various things: the piano in the hall, a bench, the length of the office, the whiteboard . . . When they have found the length of the object, they can write a number on a square of paper and tape it to the wool at precisely the right point. They should also keep a record of what each number stands for.

   When pupils return to class they can share their 'number lines'. They can challenge another pair to guess what objects the numbers on their wool refer to. If this is tricky, they could give the names of all the objects and the other group has to reason out which number refers to which object.

Give pupils extendable tape measures to find things of a certain length or to compare different parts of the school. These are a very motivational piece of equipment and they give a real opportunity to explore the cardinality of number.

Quick activities: Pegs and lifts

These two activities can be done without any equipment at all as mimes. They give pupils a sense of the order and the size of number through the movement of their own body.

Football kit

Ask all the children to stand up. Tell them they have a basket of washing at their feet and in it is the school football kit. On the back of each shirt there is a number. Pull out the goalkeeper's shirt. What number is on the back? Peg that to the left of our number lines. Now, pull out a new shirt. Where will that go? Pulling out the numbers in a random order, letting a different child choose each time will require pupils to make reasoned decisions about the positions of their numbers.

At the end, pull out some surprising numbers. "Hmm. This must be a rugby kit, this shirt says 15." "I think this must be a substitute's shirt, it says 23!". "Well, this is getting silly now. This shirt says 100. Where will we put that?"

To extend pupils' understanding, try these:

- Calculation shirts: "This one says it is half of half of a hundred!"

- Half-way shirts: "This one goes exactly half-way between 3 and 9."

- Inverse shirts: "When you add 10 to this shirt, you get 14."

- Mystery shirts: "This shirt is a square number greater than 10 but less than 30 and it's odd"

- Damaged shirts: "This shirt has three digits but one of the digits has come off in the wash. The hundreds digit is 1 and the units digit is 4 and it has to be a multiple of 3."

- Fractional shirts: "This shirt says 2 and a third but this one says 2 and a half. Which one should go on the left?"

Skyscraper lifts

Children stand up. They are going to imagine that they are skyscrapers and that their hand is a lift. Floor zero is at their feet (move hand to floor) and floor 100 (or any number you choose) is at the top of their heads (raise hands to top of heads). Some children might enjoy making a swooshing noise as the lift travels up or down and the movement of their hands may help them link the size of number with their orders. Try moving the lift with a range of questions.

- Quick-fire: Go to floor 0. Floor 100. Floor 50. Floor 51. Floor 99. Floor 10. Floor 11. . ..

- Start on zero: Go up 10. Go up 5. Go down 1. Where are you?

- Go to floor 50. Now go down 1 floor. Which floor are you on?

- Go to floor 20. The lift goes up 3 floors then down 4 floors. Where are you?

- Go to floor 20. The lift goes down 4 floors and up 3 floors. What do you notice?

- The lift goes up 10 floors. Then up another 10. How could you have done that in 1 move?

- The lift goes down 20 floors and ends up on floor 30. Where did it start?

- The lift travels down from 99 and stops on every square number floor. What is the third stop it will make?

Although both of these activities might be used with KS1 or even Reception (in a slightly simplified way) they might also easily challenge and extend the most confident pupils in KS2. All pupils will benefit from linking physical movement with the calculations they are making.

Drawing number lines usefully

Time spent teaching children the skills of drawing a number line will be invaluable. It is often tempting to give children printed number lines as they can use them as tools to get the right answer to calculations. This is perfectly understandable and may be useful for certain lessons but pupils need to develop the skills. If they are unable to draw their own accurate and useful number lines then they will not develop independent calculation skills.

There are a number of key teaching points:

- We draw them neatly because it helps calculate accurately.
- We use a ruler to draw them but we don't have to space every number out by exactly one cm. We can choose how far apart we want to put the numbers.
- We don't need to write every single number onto the number line. Often it's better to write in only the numbers that are useful for our calculation.

Give pupils regular opportunities to practise the skills needed. This can be a starter at the beginning of the day, could be on whiteboards or in exercise books. You can then focus on whether children are making decisions about what information their number line needs to show.

Investigation: Number line challenges

Draw a number line that shows:

Basic	Trickier	Challenging
All the numbers from 0 to 5	Some numbers between 1 and 2	Square/prime numbers between 50 and 100
Numbers from 20 to 30	4 different numbers greater than 1000 and less than 1002	All the factors of . . . 10 . . . 24 . . . 36 . . . 100 . . . 360
All the even numbers from 0 to 20	Multiples of 4 and multiples of 5 up to 50	$9 - 8 + 7 - 6 + 5 - 4 + 3 - 2 + 1$
The numbers in the 5 times table	Multiples of 9 greater than 90	Where you began if you ended up on 99 after adding 30 to a number then halving the answer
How to add 4 to 7	Two different ways to add 99 to a number	
How to subtract 4 from 11	The number halfway between 7 and 10	The number half way between the numbers 4.01 and the number 4.1
How much you need to add to 13 to reach 20		

These challenges can be endlessly adapted and they require pupils to make mathematical decisions at every stage. This is an excellent and easy assessment opportunity.

Reflection: How many numbers?

How many numbers on a 0–10 number line?

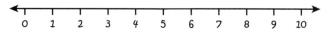

The obvious and immediate answer is 10 but when pupils count they are often surprised to find that there are in fact 11 different numbers on the number line. Why is this the case? How many numbers on a 0–100 number line?

Number lines should be used by pupils as a way of recording their thinking rather than seen as a specific tool to be used for a certain job in only a certain way. Playing 'Your guess is too big' (see below) can be adapted easily to show one way of doing this.

Quick activity: Your guess is too big

Say to the pupils that you're thinking of a number, and you think they'll NEVER guess it in a million years. The only answers you're permitted to give are: "Your guess is too big" and "Your guess is too small." While pupils guess, model how to show their answers on a number line. The pictures below demonstrate how this can be done by shading out the region that has been eliminated. Using this method, pupils will guess your number surprisingly quickly. There are a number of ways of developing this activity to make it even more surprising:

- Choose a decimal or a fraction, e.g. 2.5
- Choose a negative number
- Allow the pupils to choose the number

Discuss different strategies for guessing and which strategies should help you find any number most quickly.

Here, parts of the number line are scrubbed out as the guesses get closer and closer to the missing number. Although the number line is drawn relatively quickly and parts are scribbled out, it is still clear and useful.

Working with a range of numbers around zero, from -5 up to 5 or from -10 up to 10 will often produce more mathematical thinking and deepen understanding more than working with a line going from 0 to a million.

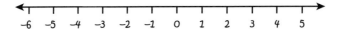

A range of simple questions about this number line can make an excellent discussion starter:

- What number is 2 less than 1?
- How many pairs can you find with a difference of 3?
- How far do you have to jump from 4 to –6.
- How many addition calculations could you show on this number line?
- 10 less than 26 is 16. 10 less than 16 is 6. What is 10 less than 6? Make sure you check your answer by counting on the number line.
- I subtracted 20 from a number and ended up on –3. What number did I start on?

Jumping on and jumping back

Practising jumping around on a number line gives a great visual/physical hook for children to hang their mental additions and subtractions from. This will give them a sense of how the calculations behave.

Reflection: How do the numbers behave on a number line?

Read the tasks below and think about the link between them and about how the second task might add or support mathematical thinking. How would your pupils approach the different tasks? Would any of them draw diagrams or would they work purely on the calculations? Can you think of any pupils who would particularly benefit from one task over another?

1 5 + 6 – 2 = ?
2 Imagine a number line. You are on number 5. You jump on 6 and then jump back 2. Where are you now?

How could you adapt the tasks to challenge more confident pupils (thinking beyond simply making the numbers larger)?

Linking the calculations with diagrams on a number line and also with the sense of actions on objects can help make sense of the process. Pupils who understand these links are more likely to be able to apply calculation strategies flexibly. It also helps to make clear how the size of numbers (cardinality) relates to the order of numbers (ordinality).

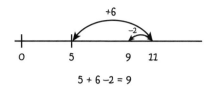

$$5 + 6 - 2 = 9$$

This number line gives pupils a mental picture for how the calculations behave as action on the numbers.

Quick activity: Leap before you look

Ask pupils to draw a blank number line with intervals marked but no numbers added to it. Now might be a good time to choose with the class a name for those little horizontal lines we use to show where the numbers will go. Next, ask the pupils to show a jump of -4 on it. Ask them to prove that their jump shows -4.

This is a good opportunity to rehearse the vocabulary for subtraction: What other ways can we say this? "Four less", "Take four away", "Take away four", "Minus four", "Subtract four",. . . "Add negative four". Now, they need to choose where to put zero on their number lines. It could go anywhere, not just at the far left. Once they have put zero in they can fill in the rest of the numbers:

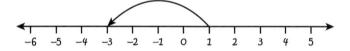

What calculation have the pupils created?

This activity can be varied for greater challenge:

- Make the scale different: each interval might be worth 0.1 or 2 or 25.
- Use fractional jumps.
- Combine jumps: show jumps for -4, +9, -3.
- Define strict criteria: Design a calculation that involves 2 jumps and begins and ends on an odd number. . .

There are a number of other useful activities that you can undertake with very basic number lines to draw out important features of different calculations:

Questions to ask	Teaching point
How many different jumps can you show for –5?	This should draw out the point that 8 – 3 is the same as 7 – 2 is the same as 6 – 1. . . This will be very useful when looking at how "Find the difference between . . . and . . ." is related to subtraction.
I jumped back 6 and landed on 13. Where did I start?	This requires pupils to work backwards and is very useful for learning about inverse operations.
What happens if you join two jumps together? Start on any number: Jump on 6 then back 7. What do you notice? Now reverse the order of the jumps: Jump back 7 then Jump on 6. What happens?	Combining jumps should help pupils see that they can use number lines flexibly, and break a calculation into smaller steps. Also, pupils will deepen their sense of how addition and subtraction are inverse operations.

The three number lines below are a very good way to show the flexibility and efficiency of number lines. Once pupils have understood how to combine jumps on a number line, these diagrams can give pupils a great insight into efficiency in calculation.

Many pupils will not automatically see that 13 + 99 can be calculated as 13 + 100 – 1 but the diagrams will help to embed the idea and to show why they work. This method is also a very fine example of how problems can be solved in different ways and how an elegant solution can often be found by thinking beyond the obvious.

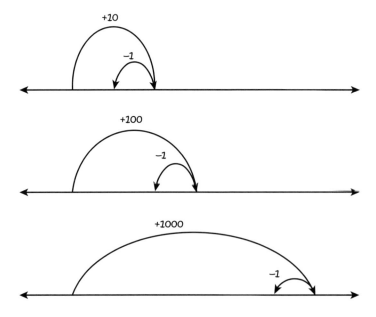

How far from x to y?

If we think of the simple calculation: 6 + 7 = 13 we may turn that into an exercise by simply hiding one of the elements:

6 + 7 = ?   What is 7 more than 6?
6 + ? = 13   What do you have to add to 6 to give 13?
? + 7 = 13   To what number do you have to add 7 to give 13?

This varies the exercise by hiding one piece of information from an equation. We might even choose to hide the operation:

6 ? 7 = 13   What operation is needed to give 13 from 6 and 7?

All of the information is encoded in a simple number line diagram:

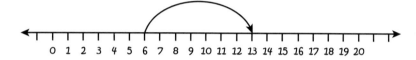

It is important to vary the information that is hidden so that pupils learn to understand the operations more deeply and to use the diagrams to support thinking not *in place* of thinking.

Discussion point: Jumping to the next 10/100/whole number. . . versus jumping on 10, 100, . . .

What are the similarities and differences in the skills needed to tackle the following problems:

- What is 10 more than 13?
- What is the next ten from 13?
- How far is it from 13 to 20?
- What is 100 more than 113?
- What is the next hundred from 113?
- How much do you have to jump from 113 to the next hundred?
- Can you show three different ways to jump from 113 to the next hundred?
- If I jump back 100 from 13, where will I arrive?
- How far from 13 to 1000?

Are any of these problems easier or more difficult than each other? If so, what makes them more or less tricky? Perhaps some people find different kinds easier than others. If so, then a discussion of methods or thought processes may help everyone deepen their understanding.

Choosing your 'stop-offs'

One way that many pupils will differ is in how they think of 'stop-offs'. When finding the size of the gap between 63 and 100, some may choose to add on 7 first, to 'stop off' at 70 before adding 30 to reach 100.

Others may choose to count on in 10s until they reach 93 then add on a final 7. Some pupils may choose to add on 11 then 80, then 5... in seemingly random jumps. There are an infinite number of solutions but some are more efficient than others, and less prone to error.

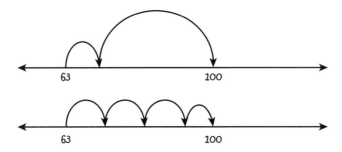

Zooming in... an infinity of numbers

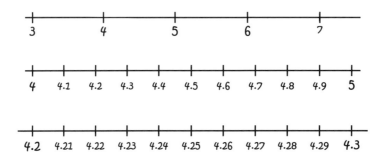

Pupils will need to be experts at number lines. It will allow them to interpret increasingly abstract ideas within number such as decimals and fractions, coordinates and graphs, scales on maps and measurements in technical drawings. The benefits of mastering number lines will pay dividends throughout education and into adult life, including a deeper understanding of number.

Harnessing the power of arrays

The activities in this section are designed to help pupils master arrays. They develop in complexity so that pupils move from action on objects, through use of pictures and symbols, to being able to visualise arrays. They also help pupils to unpick the mechanics of arrays and understand how they work – which is vital for deep conceptual understanding.

They can be used:

As starters: repeated regularly as lesson starters, the activities will help pupils maintain mastery of the skill of using arrays. Pupils should be encouraged to see the link between arrays and different topics (such as division, fractions, percentages and ratios).

As lessons: directly teaching a class to master the array is important in the Autumn term of every school year as it supports understanding of so many concepts – even as basic as times tables. Also, it is a very good way of producing striking visual work that can be displayed for the first term.

To support struggling pupils: for pupils who struggle with times tables, multiplication and division and who do not see the link between calculation methods and problem solving, this would be a good sequence of lessons to follow, either with a teacher or a TA, over a period of weeks to support their understanding and give them calculation strategies useful for a range of problems.

As time fillers: in spare 5 or 10 minute moments (before lunch, at the end of the day, during registration, waiting for everyone to change from PE) to revise and challenge all pupils.

What do we mean by arrays?

An array is an arrangement of objects or symbols in a grid into **rows** and **columns**. They are a very common human construction – think of window panes, bathroom tiles, patios, egg cartons, a phone keypad, Snakes and Ladders – but almost never seen in nature. Perhaps the closest we usually see is the pattern in a honeycomb but look closely and you will see important differences between an array and a honeycomb. An array must be arranged into rows and columns, for example a young child lining up her teddies has made an array with just one row.

Outdoor learning: Autumn arrays

Collect fallen leaves and arrange them into arrays on the playground. Agree that when the pupil has told you some information about their array you will photograph it. The fire colours of autumn leaves stand out beautifully against the dark asphalt and they become a striking classroom resource. Pupils might tell you simply that their array has 3 rows or that it has 5 rows and 8 columns or that it represents a square number because it is the same width as length.

Here are some probing questions, to get pupils to think mathematically about the arrays:

- Describe your array to me.

- How can you convince me that it is an array and not just a neat pile of leaves?

- What would you say about this array if you looked at it from this angle?

- If I want to make an array with exactly two rows, how many leaves should I collect?

- Can you make an array in a square shape that doesn't have a square number of leaves?

- How many different arrays could you make using 12 leaves? What about 13 leaves?

- How many leaves would you need to add another column to your array?

- Can you think of different ways to count all the leaves in your array?

To follow-up, back in class:
Look at the photographs in class. Have pupils discuss which calculations could be used to count the leaves. Print out small copies of the photographs, laminate them and use them as a set of array cards for the class. They can be used as starters or for practising times tables or for revision in small groups. Pupils can sort the cards into different categories (multiples of 5, arrays with an even number of leaves . . .)

Using arrays to understand number

There are many uses for arrays as pupils progress in their understanding of number. If pupils can visualise and represent arrays then it will provide a sound foundation for understanding all of proportionality (multiplication and division, fractions, times tables . . .), which is one of the most common blocks to progress. They are a good way of visualising prime numbers, factors and multiples and can be used to good effect to illustrate fractions of amounts, ratio and proportion, and percentages. The activities in the chapter build on the key strengths of the array as a physical, visual and mental representation of objects:

1 **Efficient counting:** The structure of the array helps pupils to count a number of objects by breaking the task into manageable chunks. It is akin to the way we might count all the money from a jar of change by sorting it into groups of equal size.

> Give each group of pupils a large number of objects (cubes, paperclips, counters, pebbles...) and ask them to work together to count how many there are. Look out for pupils who group them into 2s or 10s, and model how that can be represented as an array.

2 **Grouping and commutativity:** They are a strong visual cue for grouping. A 3 by 4 array shows 3 groups of 4 and also 4 groups of 3. When pupils can shift their attention between the two different ways of grouping they can get a strong sense of why 3 x 4 = 4 x 3. Also, it shows 12 divided into 4 groups or shared between 4 people. Grouping is a very important concept for thinking about counting, multiplication, division and fractions.

 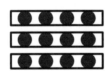

> The same array can be grouped in different ways for multiplication and division.
>
> 3 x 4 = 4 x 3

3 **New facts from old:** It is easy to add a row or column to an array and find out new facts from old ones. If you have a 10 by 3 array, you can easily add a column to make 11 x 3 or take a column away for 9 x 3. This can lead to finding out 201 x 17 if you know 200 x 17 = 3400.

> How to 'see' 11 x 3 by thinking about 10 x 3

4 **Flexible**: Arrays can be halved, partitioned, combined and adjusted to demonstrate a range of concepts and methods, and pupils can get the sense of being in control of number. It shows a 4 x 4 array doubled to make an 8 x 4 array. This way pupils can use 4 x 4 to work out 8 x 4.

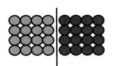

> You can split arrays into different sections to demonstrate different concepts. Here, you can show how to work out the 8 x 4 by thinking about 4 x 4.

5 **Square Numbers**: A deep conceptual understanding of square numbers will be vital as pupils progress through KS2 to algebra in KS3 and 4. The square array is a very strong image to support that understanding.

> This particular pattern shows one way of thinking about square numbers.
>
> 1 + 3 | 5 + 7 – 4 x 4
>
> Can you think of a pattern for 5 x 5?

6. **Area**: Arrays make a sound basis for understanding and calculating area, and distinguishing it from perimeter.

> We calculate the area of a rectangle by splitting it into an array. This rectangle is 6 cm by 5 cm – so we can calculate the area with 6cm x 5cm = 30cm^2

7. **Calculation methods**: Variations on the grid method are commonly used to teach the concepts of multiplication. Arrays support this very well, and also other methods involving partitioning (including column multiplication).

> By demonstrating how partitioning relates to the structure of arrays, we build pupils' concepts of long multiplication and grid method.

An efficient method of counting

Pupils will need some practise with the vocabulary of arrays and of applying them to real life and mathematical contexts. Encourage them to use the words 'row' and 'column' to describe their own arrays and to draw arrays with some care. It is also important to get pupils to feel confident about applying the mathematical notation to particular arrays. The following activity can be used to practise vocabulary and writing multiplication calculations to match different arrays.

Investigation: House arrays

Begin by showing the pupils a picture of a house with many windows (e.g. *Mr Uppity* by Roger Hargraves). Ask some questions to begin drawing out the mathematics:

How do we know this is a rich persons' house?

Can anyone think of a good way of counting all those windows?

Share ideas, and model how the windows are arranged in arrays. Draw a few different arrays, some with mistakes, and compare them. Model how to match an array with a multiplication calculation. Set a target for a number of windows – 100 is a good place to begin. Challenge pupils to design their own house with exactly that number of windows. The task can be very simply modified by altering the conditions for success:

- Design a house with lots of windows. Show the calculations you need to 'count' how many windows.

- Design a house with more than 50 windows but fewer than 100.

- Design a house with more than 50 windows in a symmetrical arrangement.

- Design a house with exactly 100 windows.

- Design a house with exactly 100 windows – use at least 2 different square numbers.

- Design a house with exactly 93 windows – using only arrays with an odd number of rows.

- Design a house with exactly 64 windows – using exactly 6 arrays, each with a different number of columns.

As a **plenary**, you can explore questions such as these:

- My window has 25 panes of glass. It has 5 rows. How many in each row? (Link with division and inverse operations).

- My window has 35 panes of glass. It is 7 rows by 5 columns. How many panes would there be if I added another row? What if I took a column away? (Finding new facts from old).

- Try drawing a window with 7 panes of glass. Describe the shapes it can be. Can you find any other numbers like that? (Link with prime numbers).

Pupils may resort to counting all the objects in the array (one at a time). This can establish which pupils are not confident in times tables or in using efficient methods for calculating. Encourage these pupils to notice that there are the same number in each row and column and to use this fact to help. For these pupils, arrays with 2, 5 or 10 in a row are the most effective to use. Pupils will need help to see that '3 x 4' is a useful way of describing an array. They may prefer to call it simply '12'. By writing the calculation we highlight the *mathematical structure* rather than just the *right answer*. Encourage pupils to use the calculation as the 'name' of the array.

Arrays and areas

It is vital for pupils that they understand the link between arrays and areas. From KS2 to KS4, pupils will be required to solve area problems and many struggle because they have simply learnt a formula by rote. By using arrays to build their concept of area pupils can develop their problem solving skills and save themselves a great deal of trouble over their school career.

Problem solving: Arrays as areas

Give each pupil a rectangle, preferably made out of coloured card or paper. It would be useful for each rectangle to be about 10cm x 7cm. For each table, give the pupils a selection of cubes and square shapes that they can use to cover the shape.

Problem solving A

- How many cubes could you fit on your rectangle?
- How many . . . could fit on your rectangle? (square shapes, stamps, multi-link cubes . . .)
- How many of your rectangles would you need to completely cover your table?
- How many of your rectangles would you need to completely cover the carpet in your classroom?

Problem solving B

- Estimate how many rectangles would need to cover a gym mat, the school hall, the ceiling of the headteacher's office.

- What could you do to check your estimates?

- Join your rectangle to someone else's to make a new rectangle. How many cubes cover your new shape?

Problem solving C

- Cut your rectangle in half to make two new rectangles. Join them together in a different way. How many cubes cover your new shape?

- How many 1 inch by 1 inch squares would cover your shape?

- What happens to the area of your shape if you cut a 1cm square out of one corner?

- What would happen to the area of your shape if you cut it in half diagonally?

Pupils will need to see that area is always measured in a chosen unit. They will be most familiar with cm² because that is an easy to use unit particularly in the classroom and in exercise books (where the squares are often neatly drawn out already). However, there are a number of units for measuring area: square inches, square feet, acres, hectares, km² and so on. When we calculate the area of a shape, really we are working out how many of a certain unit would completely cover the surface.

Discussion point: Area

Units are usually squares but occasionally we see them given as rectangles. For example, you often hear statistics like 'An area the size of 12 football pitches is cut-down every 12 seconds'.

- Why are units for area usually squares?

- Why don't we use circles to measure area?

- What other shapes could we use to measure area?

- What units can you invent?

3
Four Operations

> **Key concept**
>
> Calculation is a gateway to outstanding mathematical learning. Being able to calculate is NOT the main business of the mathematician nor for that matter the bank clerk, engineer, accountant or any other person who deals with numbers. Even before computers came along, being able to add columns of figures or perform long division on 12-digit numbers was hardly anything more than a robotic process.
>
> The main business of mathematics is thinking mathematically:
>
> - **reasoning** logically;
> - **spotting** patterns;
> - **solving** problems and puzzles;
> - **deducing** hidden information;
> - **devising** systems and efficient methods;
> - **imagining** new ways to understand the world.
>
> These skills are important for everyone, in all walks of life, irrespective of whether numbers are a part of their everyday business.

What is important about learning calculation?

- Investigation: when you can calculate, you can explore the patterns and relationships in number;
- Understanding: learning how calculations affect numbers empowers you to understand the world;
- Error-spotting: a good sense of how calculations behave will help you spot errors in finance, construction, scientific experiments, cooking and so on;
- Empowerment: journalism, advertising and political canvassing often use statistics and calculations to try to persuade you to behave in a certain way. Having a good sense of calculation will empower you to notice when figures are being manipulated;
- Self-esteem: maths is an emotive subject and having confidence with number will raise self-esteem. People who lack confidence feel disempowered and/or disengaged.

Learning mathematics at school is commonly misunderstood as being about learning to calculate. There are some reasons why it is important to develop calculation skills but calculation should not be seen as the end in itself but rather as a gateway to learning and to understanding.

Why do we learn them in pairs?

Consider the following equations:

4 + 7 = 11	4 x 7 = 28

Although these appear to be simply about addition and subtraction, they do in fact contain as much information about subtraction and division. It all depends on what bit of information is hidden. Consider the various missing number problems below and the structure of the diagrams that go with them.

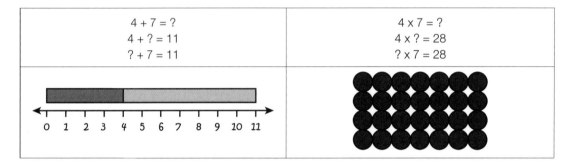

Pupils who do not learn addition with subtraction or multiplication with division will struggle to solve problems other than very straightforward calculations even if they are proficient at all the methods. They need to understand the connection.

Are subtraction and division more challenging to learn?

It certainly seems to be the case that most people struggle more with subtraction and division.

Reflection: Easy or difficult?

What makes subtraction seem more difficult? Why is division seen as harder than multiplication? Ask the pupils directly. Here are some statements that staff/pupils may agree or disagree with. They can be used as prompts for thinking and discussion:

- We learn to count up first which is like adding.
- When you subtract or divide it seems like thinking backwards.
- We have to add more often than subtract.
- It is easier to join things together than take them apart.

- Think of an easy subtraction and an easy division. What makes them easy?
- Write an example of a tricky addition and a tricky multiplication. What makes them tricky?
- Is it to do with the pictures you make in your head?

What are the solutions to this?

- Spend more time practising the harder skills;
- Spend more time learning them as inverse operations;
- Spend more time developing understanding of the concepts.

All of these suggestions seem sensible. The activities in this chapter aim to give pupils the chance to develop their understanding in a way that does not simply give them more and more examples to try with larger and larger numbers. There are two ways to vary how we learn a skill:

1. Variations within an activity.

2. The same skill applied in a variety of ways.

Building in pattern and structure to an activity gives pupils more opportunity to understand the behaviour of calculations than a random sample of exercises.

Quick activity: How are they connected?

These calculations are designed so that pupils can pick out patterns and generalities. The idea is that they spark pupils' understanding of how the numbers behave.

Exercise 1	Exercise 2	Exercise 3	Exercise 4
$101 - 9 = ?$	$100 - ? = 51$	$? - 9 = 101$	$30 \div ? = 3$
$201 - 9 = ?$	$200 - ? = 51$	$? - 9 = 201$	$60 \div ? = 3$
$301 - 9 = ?$	$300 - ? = 51$	$? - 9 = 301$	$120 \div ? = 3$
$401 - 9 = ?$	$400 - ? = 51$	$? - 9 = 401$	$240 \div ? = 3$
$1001 - 9 = ?*$	$1000 - ? = 51*$	$? - 9 = 1001*$	$2400 \div ? = 3*$
$1002 - 9 = ?*$	$1001 -? = 51*$	$? - 9 = 1002*$	$2403 \div ? = 3*$
. . .	. . .	. . .	. . .

Notice how the calculations in each exercise are all related. The subtraction exercises build on increasing patterns. Look at how exercise 1 is related to exercise 3. In the division example (exercise 4) a pattern of doubling is used as this builds in proportional reasoning. Notice also how there is a jump to the final two exercises (marked *) so that pupils have to notice the general pattern and not just mechanically fill in information.

Multiple solutions and more challenging missing information

I have already discussed how to vary an exercise so that the hidden information (the 'answer') is in different places. Even something as simple as changing $23 + ? = 30$ to $30 = ? + 23$ keeps pupils thinking mathematically. A good way to increase the challenge of an exercise is to increase how much information is hidden. For example, compare:

a) $10 = ? + 1$

b) $10 = ? + ? + 1$

There is only one solution to (a) though there is more than one way to find that solution. There are many solutions to (b) however, and the level of mathematical thinking required is greatly increased.

Problem solving: Many solutions

These problems can be done using pencil and paper or on whiteboards. However, they can be given an extra dimension by drawing each problem on a strip of cardboard so that pupils can use a set of digit cards to find different solutions. This introduces the idea of exchange. A pupil might have $10 - 3 + 4 = 11$. If they change the 3 card for a 2 card, then they might notice that they can decrease the 4 card by 1 as well to have $10 - 2 + 3$. Using digit cards like this can help pupils begin to understand how equations behave.

$? + ? + 9 = 20$	$? + ? + ? + ? = 15$	$10 - ? + ? = 11$	$2 = ? + ? + ?$

The challenge can be adapted in a number of ways:

- Use only single digits.
- Should repeats be allowed?
- Find more than 3 solutions.
- Does a different order represent a different solution? e.g. is $5 + 6 + 9 = 20$ different from $6 + 5 + 9 = 20$?
- Aim to find all possible solutions.
- Allow decimal/fractional/negative numbers.
- Make certain specific conditions: use at least one odd number/use only odd numbers/use a square number. . .

All pupils can access these problems and all can find a level of challenge. A confident pupil might spend a whole lesson investigating why none of the examples can be solved using only odd numbers and then inventing a range of problems that can be solved using exactly one even and one odd number. Further challenges:

- Can they be solved using only prime numbers?
- Can they be solved using numbers with 1 decimal place (e.g. 2.5, 3.4, 17.2) without repeating a digit?

Here are a range of further exercises like this. Some of these require an understanding that the equals sign represents a kind of balancing point, that = means 'is equivalent to' and not 'here comes the answer'.

Easier	Medium	Tricky
? + ? + 10 = 20	10 = 1 + ? + 8 − ?	20 x ? = ? − 20
? + ? + ? + ? = 20	? − ? + 1 = 10	? x 5 = 100 ÷ ?
20 = 1 + ? + 10 + ?	? x ? − 4 = 20	10 x ? − 1 = ? + 10

Addition and subtraction

+	1	2	3	4	5	6	7	8	9	10
1	2	3	4	5	6	7	8	9	10	11
2	3	4	5	6	7	8	9	10	11	12
3	4	5	6	7	8	9	10	11	12	13
4	5	6	7	8	9	10	11	12	13	14
5	6	7	8	9	10	11	12	13	14	15
6	7	8	9	10	11	12	13	14	15	16
7	8	9	10	11	12	13	14	15	16	17
8	9	10	11	12	13	14	15	16	17	18
9	10	11	12	13	14	15	16	17	18	19
10	11	12	13	14	15	16	17	18	19	20

This addition square shows just how rich in pattern addition and subtraction are. Pupils will enjoy unpicking the patterns in these diagrams, for example how the units change in each column or how numbers appear in diagonals. To be able to add and subtract, pupils need very little. We can perform 12 + 29 by collecting a pile of 12 pebbles and a pile of 29 pebbles, then counting them all. We could perform 29 − 12 using pebbles and counting as well.

Discussion points: Pebbles for addition and subtraction

Which of the following calculations could be solved using pebbles? What are the difficulties in using the pebble counting methods for some of them:

- 324249 + 2628917
- 21 + 4

- 21 − 4
- 4 − 21
- 2½ + 5½
- 13 − 2½
- 2.1 − 1.05
- 7 + 99
- 100000001 + 100000002 + 100000003 + 100000004

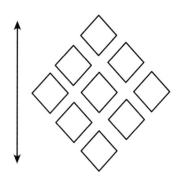

Pupils could discuss this as a 'Diamond 9' activity. Each calculation is written on a piece of paper or card and then arranged into the pattern. The simpler the calculation, the nearer the top of the pattern it should go. This kind of activity gives pupils the opportunity to think about how calculations can be tackled without having to actually solve them. In this way, pupils will gain an insight into their own ideas about calculation and get to hear other people's methods or ideas. It is a very good opportunity to observe pupils and make assessments about their conceptual understanding. This gives a different kind of assessment than seeing if they have the right answer or not or looking at their workings.

In this particular discussion, focused on the pebble method, the pupils should decide which calculations best suit pebbles, not which are easiest to find the answer to. But, once they have discussed and agreed the positions and justified their decisions you can change the criteria:

- Now the ones nearer the top need to be the ones that are easier to solve mentally. Do any cards need to move now? Do any stay in the same position?

- What about if we sort them based on how easy they are to solve with column methods or on a number line?

- Now sort them based on the units digit of the answer. You can work out the first card has a 6 in the units place without working out the whole answer.

Look out for pupils who can really analyse the demands of the calculations for different methods. Some pupils may be used to churning out calculations but not thinking about efficient methods and these pupils may find it difficult to notice if an error has crept into their workings.

Learning how to add and subtract is more than simply knowing how to find answers to calculations. It is about:

- Noticing errors or inaccuracies;
- Understanding how different methods relate to one another;
- Noticing how the methods reflect the actual idea of increase and decrease;
- Applying calculations to solve problems and puzzles;
- Choosing efficient methods based on the numbers.

Investigation: Flexible partitioning

Give pupils 5 interlocking cubes (or 5 counters in a row). Tell them to break the cubes up into parts, so that they may have 2 cubes and 3 cubes.

How many ways can you find of splitting 5 cubes into 'parts' or 'chunks'? Before beginning, make an estimate: Do pupils think there are more than 10 ways? Various questions will come up:

- Are you allowed 5 on its own? (Yes)
- Does 2 + 3 count as different from 3 + 2? (No – although this could be changed later for an extension task)
- Can you split it into more than 2 parts e.g. 1 + 2 + 2? (Yes)

The challenge is to see if pupils can convince you and themselves that they have found all the possible solutions.

There are 7 different solutions:

- 5 (1 part);
- 1 + 4, 2 + 3 (2 parts);
- 1 + 1 + 3, 1 + 2 + 2 (3 parts)
- 1 + 1 + 1 + 2 (4 parts);
- 1 + 1 + 1 + 1 + 1 (5 parts).

You can model how to collect the different solutions and how to use an organised system (like always starting with the smallest part) so you can see if you have repeated any solutions. Pupils might like to use a symbolic recording system or actual cubes themselves.

Next steps

- Try to find how many parts you can split 3 cubes into, 4 cubes into, 6 cubes into, . . . up to 10 cubes.
- How many different solutions are there for 4 cubes if 1 + 3 is different from 3 + 1?
- How many different partitions of 70 cubes, if you can only split them into multiples of 10 e.g. (10 + 30 + 30)

Partitioning of a number is often taught as splitting it into its hundreds, tens and units digits: 372 becomes 300 + 70 + 2. This is a useful technique as it links with the place value system for our numbers but it can set up a rigid kind of thinking. Flexible partitioning, where the pupils feel able to split a number into whatever parts best suit the calculation, will be a very useful technique for all four operations.

List all the ways of partitioning 70 into two parts: 10 + 60, 20 + 50, . . . Now discuss with pupils how these partitions can be used to find the answers to the following additions and subtractions. These can be solved without thinking about the partitions we created at the beginning but the focus of this is how that flexible partitioning can be used.

80 + 70	130 – 70	80 + 71
180 + 70	230 – 70	180 + 71
280 + 70	330 – 70	130 – 71
380 + 70	630 – 70	230 – 71
980 + 70	1030 – 70	1030 – 71

A number line is a useful model for this:

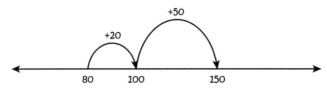

Decimal place value

There are a number of ways of presenting place value to pupils. The boxes diagram below draws out the pattern of repeating hundreds tens and units as we move through the thousands, millions, billions. . . This pattern helps pupils understand the vocabulary of our number system.

Trillion			Billion			Million			Thousand					
H	T	1	H	T	1	H	T	1	H	T	1	H	T	1

Many pupils struggle knowing what the 5 represents in 53876, for example, and they can use the boxes to see how the digits fit into the number system.

Trillion			Billion			Million			Thousand					
H	T	1	H	T	1	H	T	1	H	T	1	H	T	1
										5	3	8	7	6

The 5 in the tens box of the thousands group is worth 5 lots of ten thousand which is 50,000.

only produce the digits 1–6. Pupils can make their own 0–9 spinners by splitting a decagon into 10 triangles. The process of making the spinner can be made more or less challenging but it is a good exercise in its own right. Some pupils could even construct the decagon from scratch using a protractor to measure precise angles.

To use the spinner, make a hole in the centre. Spin a paperclip around the point of a pencil held upright over the central hole to select a random digit.

There are a number of decisions that pupils may consider:

- Will the order of the digits make a difference?

- Will they write just the digit in the gaps, or make a dotty pattern akin to those on dice? What will the pattern of dots look like for 7, 8 and 9?

- Do they know numbers in any other languages that could be added to the spinner?

To ensure that the spinners last a long time, they can be laminated for protection. Pupils are then able to write on them with whiteboard pens and make any changes. There are a number of random digit games to be played which can develop pupils' reasoning about number. Here are just a few:

- Who can generate the largest 4 digit number?

- Spin 5 random digits. What is the smallest 4 digit odd number you can make? What is the second largest even number you can make?

- Who can generate the number closest to . . .?

- Who can create an addition of three 3 digit numbers (see below) with an answer as close to 1000 as possible?

You can create endless variations of this with different numbers of digits and different target numbers. Pupils are motivated by the random nature of the digits.

With random digits, pupils tend to want to get the highest score. Mixing up the challenges so that sometimes they have to hope for smaller digits or specific digits will help them approach problem-solving activities with an open mind.

Investigation: Digital roots

Teaching pupils about how to find the digital root of a number is a good context for addition and for developing an understanding of number. To find the digital root of a number is simple: you simply add up all the digits.

Below are some examples:

$32 \rightarrow 3 + 2 \rightarrow 5$. . . the digital root of 32 is 5.
$71 \rightarrow 7 + 1 \rightarrow 8$. . . the digital root of 71 is 8.

If you add the digits and they sum to more than a single digit, then you repeat the process until you are left with a single digit. For example:

$78 \rightarrow 7 + 8 \rightarrow 15 \rightarrow 1 + 5 \rightarrow 6$. . . The digital root of 78 is 6.
$9677 \rightarrow 9 + 6 + 7 + 7 \rightarrow 29 \rightarrow 2 + 9 \rightarrow 11 \rightarrow 1 + 1 \rightarrow 2$. . . The digital root of 9677 is 2.

There are many interesting patterns in digital roots. Begin by exploring the digital roots of the 9 times table. Then try the 3 times table. After that, you might ask your own questions, like 'Is there a pattern in the digital roots of the square numbers?' or 'What would a 100 square look like if I wrote the digital root of each number in a grid?'. These are the kinds of question a mathematician asks.

Inverse operations (addition and subtraction)

Many pupils will need to develop their sense of how addition and subtraction are related and of what it means for these to be an inverse operation.

Investigation (group): That's torn it!

Each child needs a sheet of rectangular paper. Rough paper is best for this, though it needs to have at least one blank side to write on. Ask each child to tear their piece of paper into two. On each piece they should write a number within a certain range (chosen depending on the confidence of the pupils). Pupils should try to place the two torn pieces together to form the rectangle again. Find the total of the numbers on the two halves and this gives you an equation.

$17 + 24 = 41$

You might want to think of a context for this, to help visualise. Perhaps the numbers represent how many sheep are in that part of a field. The pupils might even want to draw dots or symbols to represent those objects. Now, the pupils could reverse the order to find a new fact:

$24 + 17 = 41$.

Once pupils are convinced that the total is the same whichever order, you can take one of the pieces away (hide one behind your back) and come up with subtractions to match:

$41 - 17 = 24, 41 - 24 = 17$

This is a lovely way to visualise how addition and subtraction are related to the total. Once pupils have found addition and subtraction facts for their pieces of paper they can exchange one of their pieces with someone else and create four new facts. There are many variations on this activity:

- Use larger/smaller/decimal/fractional numbers.

- Create a class set where all the pairs total 100. Deal the parts out randomly and pupils have to find their partner. This can be a good way to put pupils into random pairs.
- Tear a rectangle into 3 or more pieces. How many different facts can you create by jumbling the order and taking pieces away?

Column addition and subtraction

Computers, robots, calculators and phones can be programmed fairly simply to add and subtract using a process like column methods. No calculator yet can be said to 'understand' addition and subtraction. Pupils, too, can learn the process. There are many pupils who learn the process without understanding how it works, why it works, or how it relates to the numbers we experience through objects, measurement or pure mathematical contexts.

Reflection: Is learning maths like learning tennis?

Imagine a five year-old who wants to learn tennis. Before they are given a racquet and a ball, they are not forced to learn all the scoring system, how sidespin affects the flight of the ball due to air resistance or the comparisons between serve-volley and baseline-slogging strategies. That young child instead is encouraged to hit the ball around the garden.

- To what extent is this relevant to how we teach calculation methods?
- What must a pupil understand before they learn column addition/subtraction?
- Think of three pupils in your class. Do they all understand number and calculation in the same way? Should they learn the methods at the same time, or at different times? How would you decide?

There is a balance to be found. If we held off from teaching a calculation method until we felt a pupil had fully understood all the underlying mathematical concepts, then almost no one would ever move on to anything. Learning the process of column methods can give pupils the opportunity to experience addition and subtraction, to solve calculations and to apply their methods to problem solving contexts. However, a pupil who regularly returns to how the methods work and why, and who has a good grounding in the behaviour of numbers will be far better placed to retain their understanding and to be able to apply the methods accurately.

Investigation: From flexible partitioning to column methods

Flexible partitioning is at the heart of column methods. Let us take the number 365. As well as being a familiar number, it can be partitioned in a number of ways:

300 + 60 + 5
5 + 60 + 300

5 + 300 + 60
4 + 300 + 61
2 + 2 + 160 + 141 + 29 + 31
1 + 1 + 1 + 1+. . .

Column addition

In a way, this is like recombining partitions:

Expanded method

219	=	200	+	10	+	9
156	=	100	+	50	+	6
219 + 156	=	300	+	60	+	15
	=	375				

Column method

```
                            1
    2   1   9            2   1   9
+   1   5   6        +   1   5   6
  ─────────────        ─────────────
    3   0   0            3   7   5
        6   0
        1   5
      ─────────
    3   7   5
```

Column subtraction

Column subtraction can be thought of as a way of picking the simplest partitions to work with.

321 − 153

Method A

321	=	300	+	20	+	1			
153	=	100	+	50	+	3			
321	=	300	+	10	+	11			
153	=	100	+	50	+	3			
321	=	200	+	110	+	11			
153	=	100	+	50	+	3			
321 − 153	=	100	+	60	+	8	=	168	

Method B

```
       ²3   ¹¹2   ¹1
   −    1    5    3
      ─────────────────
        1    6    8
```

An effective way of using this is as a lesson starter is to see if pupils can spot the specific error in the workings of the same calculation performed using different methods.

Why are there two different answers to this subtraction? Where's the error?

525 – 377

Method A

525	=	500	+	20	+	5
377	=	300	+	70	+	7
425	=	400	+	110	+	15
377	=	300	+	70	+	7
525–377	=	100	+	40	+	8	=	148

Method B

$$\begin{array}{r} {}^{4}5 \quad {}^{12}2 \quad {}^{1}5 \\ -\quad 3 \quad 7 \quad 7 \\ \hline 1 \quad 5 \quad 8 \end{array}$$

If pupils can understand the bridge and see how flexible partitioning is used they will develop a deeper understanding. Returning to the how and the why, and comparing the expanded version with the column method frequently, will help maintain pupils' understanding. It is another simple form of variation, a way of keeping the pupils' brains ticking over, rather than simply programming like robots. Also, pupils who struggle with the concepts of 'carrying', 'borrowing' or 'exchanging' will need to develop a sense of how these come from flexible partitioning of numbers.

Problem solving: Column calculations

This builds on the quick activity – Beat the Calculator (p11). This can help pupils see the patterns within the column methods themselves, like lifting up the bonnet to look at the engine of a car.

. . .	. . .	. . .	. . .
a) 31 + 32 + 33 + 34	a) 19 + 29 + 39	a) 2020 – 101	a) 99 – 25
b) 41 + 42 + 43 + 44	b) 109 + 209 + 309	b) 3030 – 101	b) 909 – 25
c) 51 + 52 + 53 + 54	c) 1009 + 2009 + 3009	c) 4040 – 101	c) 9009 – 25
d) ????	d) ????	d) ????	d) ????
. . .	. . .	. . .	. . .
j). . . z). . .	j). . . z). . .	j). . . z). . .	j). . . z). . .

Each of these contains a pattern and pupils can find the structure. It will be easiest for pupils to understand the behaviour of the numbers if they write each as a column method. Once they have seen the pattern they will want to continue it. Below are some problem-solving questions that encourage mathematical thinking beyond simply churning out digits:

● Would the answer to d be greater than 1000? Can you figure it out without having to work out the calculation?

- Estimate what the 10ᵗʰ calculation in the series (calculation j) would be.
- Can you work out the answer to calculation z?
- What would the units digit of the 100ᵗʰ calculation be?
- What would be the calculation above a?
- Which calculation in the list do you predict would give an answer close to 1 000 000?
- How much more is the answer to b than the answer to a? How much more is the answer to c than to b? How much more is the answer to d than to c? Is there a pattern here as well?

Once pupils have started to develop accurate column methods, they can use them to investigate addition and subtraction themselves. Rather than simply churning out answers, pupils can explore the methods and the behaviour of numbers and digits, and deepen their understanding. Also, these activities will give the teacher an excellent opportunity to spot where some pupils are making errors.

Problem solving: Target boxes

Pupils could try these with specific digit cards or using their random digit spinners (p63).

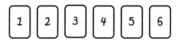

The aim is to arrange digits in the boxes so that the calculation reaches as close to the target as possible. This activity encourages mathematical thinking as the target is often not made exactly so the pupils must approximate and re-arrange digits. They have to think carefully of the effect that swapping or moving certain digits has on the final answer to the calculation.

TARGET 1000

The examples below use 6 boxes but any number can be used. These examples show how the exercise can be varied very simply, in terms of the challenge and the visual structure. It is not necessary but many pupils will respond to using actual digit cards to move around to make different calculations and this will allow them to get a sense of swapping digits for different effects.

TARGET 150

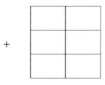

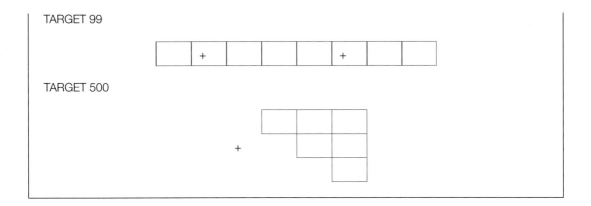

TARGET 99

TARGET 500

Once pupils have developed the basic skills of column methods, they can learn to generalise the techniques to numbers of any size.

Investigation: VLNs (Very Large Numbers) in calculation

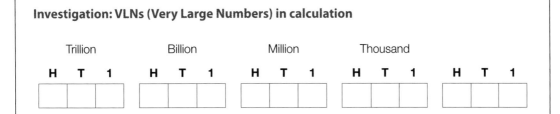

Trillion			Billion			Million			Thousand					
H	T	1	H	T	1	H	T	1	H	T	1	H	T	1

Using the idea of the boxes from their work on place value, pupils can now develop their skill so that they can compute with VLNs (very large numbers). It is best to introduce this with patterns of digits so that pupils can get a sense of how certain digit combinations cause carrying or exchanging.
Here are some good starters:

- 123 456 789 + 111 111 111
- 987 654 321 − 111 111 111
- 111 111 111 111 + 222 222 222 222 + 333 333 333 + 444 444 444
- ? + 111 111 111 = 1 000 000 000
- 987 654 321 − ? = 123 456 789
- 101 010 101 010 + ? = 1 000 000 000 000

Using VLNs can be very motivational and empowering for children and with these types of calculations, pleasing and surprising patterns occur. Some pupils will enjoy setting challenges of this kind for themselves and others. You can give them certain conditions to help them focus. The ones below are just examples:

- Use every digit 0–9 no more than twice.
- Use only odd digits or even digits for each number.
- Create a subtraction with an answer greater than 50 billion and in the five times table.

Complements to...10, 100, 1000 ...

Knowing how to find number complements is a practical skill (finding change, using percentages, using metric scales) and very useful for a range of calculation methods. It is worth spending some time as a class exploring how number complements work in our place value system.

$$2 + ? = 10$$
$$22 + ? = 100$$
$$222 + ? = 1000$$

A common misconception is to think that the number bonds to 10 prevail over all the digits in this kind of skill. That is, they think every column has to sum to ten so instead of adding 78 to 22, they add 88 to bring each column up to 10. Errors such as: $22 + 88 = 100$ are often seen and creep into the workings of longer problems. Discuss this kind of error directly with your class and give it a name: 'The Over Complement' or 'Forgotten 90s' any name will help the class remember and be a useful prompt for marking and feedback. The general rule can be found through a straightforward investigation but to refine children's understanding, slight twists on the problem can be very effective.

- Once you know how to find the complements of a number to 100, how can you find the complements to 101 or 110?
- What are the number complements to 1?

Questions with a digit missing in each column are excellent for developing awareness of complements:

$$\boxed{?}\,7 + 2\,\boxed{?} = 1\ 0\ 0$$

$$\boxed{?}\,8 + 2\,\boxed{?} = 1\ 0\ 0$$

$$\boxed{?}\,8 + 3\,\boxed{?} = 1\ 0\ 0$$

$$\boxed{?}\,7\ 6 + 1\,\boxed{?}\,2 + 4\ 1\,\boxed{?} = 1\ 0\ 0\ 0$$

$$\boxed{?}\,7\ 6 + 1\,\boxed{?}\,2 + 4\ 1\,\boxed{?} = 1\ 0\ 0\ 1$$

$$\boxed{?}\,7\ 6 + 1\,\boxed{?}\,2 + 4\ 1\,\boxed{?} = 1\ 1\ 1\ 0$$

Making adjustments

Column methods are not the final point of learning to calculate. They are useful and efficient but they are to be used as we see fit. Pupils should feel that they are in control and can apply their knowledge in innovative ways. The activity opposite demonstrates a way of adapting calculation methods to the context and the numbers involved.

Opportunities to practise the skill in a genuine context such as adding up house points or costs for class equipment or how much backing paper is needed for a certain display will also motivate pupils to see the importance of accuracy. Below are some further possible contexts for real-life calculations:

- Costing a school trip;
- Listing the equipment needed for sports day;
- Totalling the takings from a school fair or fundraising event;
- Weekly attendance.

Find the difference

Many pupils are taught that subtraction is the same as 'finding the difference' or 'counting on from the smaller number to the larger'. This is not quite accurate but it is true that subtractions can be solved using a 'find the difference method'. Often, finding the difference is the most intuitive way of calculating a subtraction, when finding change for example or working out how long until lunch. Time spent exploring the link between subtraction and finding the difference will really help pupils embed the skill. First, let us think about some ways of representing the subtraction calculation 83 − 57. In our heads, the nature of the calculation can depend very much on the context:

- A sunflower was 57cm tall last week but now it is 83 cm. How much has it grown?
- A small shrub was 83cm tall but the top 57cm were pruned away. How tall is it now?
- I saved £83 and spent £57 on a new tent. How much have I got left?
- I want to buy a tent for £83. So far I have managed to save £57. How much more do I need to save?
- $83 - ? = 57$
- $83 - 57 = ?$

Depending on how we phrase the problem, there appears to be two ways to solve it:

1. Take 57 away from 83.
2. Count up from 57 to 83.

We can help pupils understand the link by thinking about the size of the numbers (cardinality) as well as the order (ordinality). This number line represents taking away 57 from 83.

We can also represent this using bars to represent the size of each number. In this representation, a number the size of 57 is taken away from a number the size of 83. To work out how much is left we can use the order of the numbers by counting back 57 from 83.

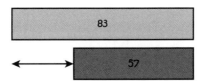

A little thought will show that actually the 57 can be taken away from the beginning, the end or even the middle of the 83. In the case where the 57 is taken away from the left hand side, we have 'a find the difference' version of the calculation. Now, the answer can be worked out by counting up to 83 from 57.

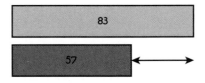

In both cases, the answer to the calculation is the size of the gap left over which clearly has to be the same size.

To link the ideas using a number line representation, the pupils can draw their own versions where the part being taken away is 'scrubbed out' from zero as the examples below demonstrate.

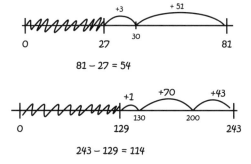

$$81 - 27 = 54$$

$$243 - 129 = 114$$

Method of equivalent difference

An understanding of the above technique for linking subtraction and find the difference can lead to a very efficient method of subtracting.

Discussion points: Equivalent differences families

Use cubes or counters for this activity. Make a line of 23 cubes, and a line of 7 underneath. If they are lined up then you can use them to find the difference between 23 and 7.

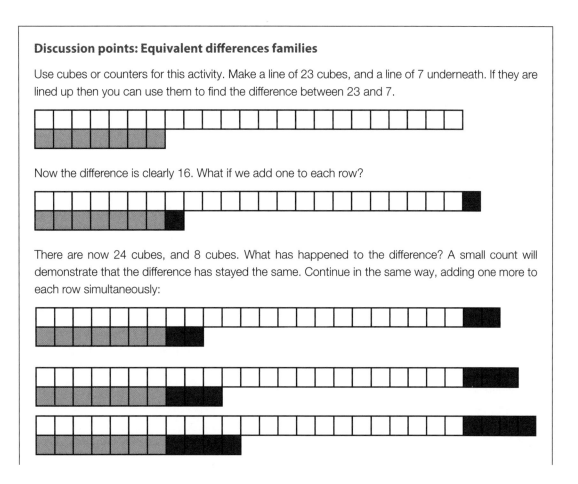

Now the difference is clearly 16. What if we add one to each row?

There are now 24 cubes, and 8 cubes. What has happened to the difference? A small count will demonstrate that the difference has stayed the same. Continue in the same way, adding one more to each row simultaneously:

You can model all of these as a family of calculations:

$23 - 7 = 16$
$24 - 8 = 16$
$25 - 9 = 16$
$26 - 10 = 16$
$27 - 11 = 16$

. . .

You can also write:

$23 - 7 = 24 - 8 = 25 - 9 = 26 - 10 = 27 - 11. . .$

Challenge pupils to come up with other 'families', and to list all of the calculations. They could photograph the cube rows as evidence and create a family gallery or colour them on squared paper. Once pupils have created them, show them a family without the answer written, for example:

$54 - 18$
$55 - 19$
$56 - 20$
$57 - 21$
$58 - 22$

Which member of this family is the easiest to complete? Scanning down the list, it seems that $56 - 20$ is straightforward to solve mentally. Once we have worked the answer out to that, then we can work out the answer to the rest of the family.

By exploring families of calculation like these, pupils can start to develop a method of equivalent differences where adjusting both parts of the subtraction allow you to solve the problem mentally. Below are some examples of how this can work and possible ways of writing it down. Allow pupils to see different examples and encourage them to understand how it links with number complements. The key is to notice that you have to add the same number to both parts of the subtraction and concentrate on making the number you take away a round number.

42 − 28	**57 − 39**	**83 − 57**	**231 − 128**	**712 − 484**
43 − 29	58 − 40	+3 +3	+2 +2	+6 +6
44 − 20		86 − 60	233 − 130	718 − 490
				+10 +10
				728 − 500
42 − 28 = 24	57 − 39 = 18	83 − 57= 26	231 − 128 = 103	712 − 484 = 228

Some pupils might use brackets to make the process clearer.
$162 - 58$
$= (162 + 2) - (58 + 2)$
$= 164 - 60$
$= 104$

Understanding the difference between addition and multiplication

Reflection: Which came first?

Children almost always learn how to add before they learn to multiply. Why is this?

- Is adding easier?

- Is it because counting and adding are linked?

- Is adding more useful?

- Or is it just the traditional approach that no one really thinks about?

Ask your pupils: Why do people learn adding before multiplying? Given the space and encouragement for deep thinking, your pupils will have some surprising and powerful insights into questions like this.

We might argue that counting is really the 1x table, and that we should learn multiplication before addition. Many of the common blocks to progress are due to problems with understanding how multiplication affects a vast number of topics. Consider the following areas which many pupils find difficult:

- Division

- Fractions

- Percentages

- Decimals

- Ratio and proportionality

- And, into later mathematics: trigonometry, similarity and congruence . . .

Many of the areas that tend to hold back understanding are due to a lack of confidence in how proportional relationships behave – at its heart: multiplication. Perhaps there's a case for increasing the amount of effort we put into learning multiplication and about all its patterns. There is more to multiplication than just times tables – it is filled with beautiful patterns for pupils to discover! Here are just a few starting points that will prompt discussion, insight, surprise, delight and understanding.

Investigation: Multiplication patterns

A multiplication square is rich with pattern and structure. Here are some activities that will encourage pupils to look and think deeply:

- What pattern do you get when you colour in all the odds?

- Colour all the multiples of 4 yellow. Now colour all the numbers 1 more than a multiple of 4 (e.g. 21 is 1 more than 20) in blue. What do you notice?

- Colour in all the square numbers.
- Colour all the squares that contain a digit '1' (e.g. 12, 81). Now try the same for '2'. Do you notice any patterns?
- Look at the patterns of just the units digits for each column.
- What are the most and least common numbers on the grid?
- What is the most common digit on the grid?
- Colour in the 3x table. Now look for all the numbers that are double the 3x table. What do you notice?
- Write out the square using the digital root of each answer e.g. 35 → 3 + 5 → 8

1	2	3	4	5	6	7	8	9	10
2	4	6	8	10	12	14	16	18	20
3	6	9	12	15	18	21	24	27	30
4	8	12	16	20	24	28	32	36	40
5	10	15	20	25	30	35	40	45	50
6	12	18	24	30	36	42	48	54	60
7	14	21	28	35	42	49	56	63	70
8	16	24	32	40	48	56	64	72	80
9	18	27	36	45	54	63	72	81	90
10	20	30	40	50	60	70	80	90	100

- Where would you find the 11x table? What about the 20x table?
- How many numbers are in the same place on a hundred square and a multiplication square?
- Find the total of each row. Can you predict the total of the next row?
- Which diagonals contain odd numbers?
- Compare the same square on both a 100 square and a multiplication square. Which contains the larger number? If you look at the same square (let's say the one at the bottom right) then you can compare the numbers. If you compare this square you will see that on the 100 square and the multiplication square, they are both 100. There are no squares where the multiplication number is larger which is a counter-intuitve idea for some.

There are endless possibilities. When a pupil spots a pattern, encourage them to think what might be causing it and to try to describe it to someone else. For an extra challenge, they can try to explain it without pointing or using any hand gestures, even while sitting back to back with their partner.

There are a number of topics where pupils need to move between addition and multiplication quite freely. Pupils need to learn both types of skill and to be able to apply them in tandem. To work out the area of this shape, pupils will need to split it into rectangles first then use multiplication to find the area of each rectangle and then add the results of the multiplications. Helping pupils to notice this kind of problem, and to apply the correct operations to the right parts of the problem means they will need to understand much more than just how to perform the calculations.

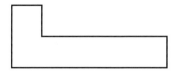

Here are four kinds of problem that involve both additive and multiplicative reasoning (including subtraction and division, of course):

- Cost reduced by a fraction or a percentage in a sale e.g. cost of a £50 jumper with 25% off.
- Area of composite shapes e.g. any L shaped hexagon (see diagram opposite).
- Total cost of multiple items: e.g. buy a football kit of socks, shorts and shirts for each player in a tem.
- Legs in a field. There are some cows and ostriches in a field. In total there are 30 legs. How many of each animal could there be? How many different solutions are there?

We have looked in Chapter 2 at arrays which are also a very good representation to support pupils' understanding of the link between multiplication and division.

Double and half

Pupils tend to have an intuitive grasp of what double and half means but that sense can get lost once they have to apply the skills to the abstract concepts of number. Again, the idea of flexible partitioning is important here and it is a good way of consolidating the link between addition and multiplication. Look at how these simple diagrams can represent partitioning and recombining for doubling and halving.

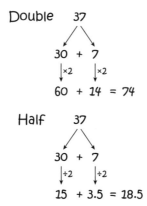

The problems that pupils often encounter can be supported by encouraging flexible partitioning – split the number up into parts that are useful to *you* for *this* calculation. Pupils who struggle to understand how these diagrams relate to the numbers will need to experience doubling objects and pictures, through the use of counters and cubes. In the diagrams below, pupils can start to see and experience how and why double 13 is the same as double 10 + double 3.

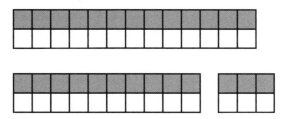

Pupils can also use counters or cubes to start to get a sense of how to halve 13 by thinking of it as 12 objects plus 1 object.

1 10 100 1000 100 10 1

A very simple variation of this exercise can embed the skill of a particular type of calculation. Look at how the following sequence of calculations contains shifting patterns, and how the missing information is presented in different places:

7 x 1 = ?	7 x 2 = ?	7 x ? = 7000	7 x ? = 28	3500 = 7 x ?
7 x 10 = ?	70 x 2 = ?	7 x ? = 700	70 x ? = 280	3500 ÷ ? = 700
7 x 100 = ?	700 x 2 = ?	7 x ? = 70	700 x ? = 2800	3500 ÷ 70 = ?
7 x 1000 = ?	7000 x 2 = ?	? x 7 = 70	7000 x ? = 28 000	35 000 ÷ ? = 7
7000 x 1 = ?	7 x 2000 = ?	? x 70 = 700	7 x ? = 28 000	3500 ÷ ? = 70
700 x 1 = ?	7 x 200 = ?	? x 700 = 7000	7 x ? = 2800	350 ÷ ? = 70
70 x 1 = ?	7 x 20 = ?	? x 70 = 7000	7 x ? = 280	? ÷ 70 = 500

There are some misconceptions that pupils commonly generate which can be tackled through the use of exercises such as these. A common error is the 'counting zeroes' error e.g. 50 x 40 = 200. Pupils make this error by making an inappropriate generalisation that the number of zeroes has to be the same on either side of the equals sign. Pupils can work through the family of facts, from the parent 5 x 4 = 20 to 50 x 4 = 200 to 50 x 40 = 2000, and in this way come to understand the correct generalisation more fully.

Grouping and sharing

In the discussion of arrays in Chapter 2, we looked at how they can be used to represent the idea of grouping as it relates to multiplication. The link between grouping and sharing is vital for developing an understanding of division.

Problem solving: Card games

Playing cards are a good context for applying the concepts of grouping and sharing. Below are two ideas to be used with the class.

Memory game/pairs

Arrange the cards into a rectangular array and then play pairs (each player turns over 2 at a time, and keeps them if they are a pair). Pupils can begin with a different number of cards (providing there is a pair for each card). To reinforce the idea of grouping, pupils could follow a rule so that the cards always have to be arranged in an array e.g. when a pair is removed from a 6 x 5 array, the pupils will have to rearrange the 28 remaining cards into an array (7 x 4 or 14 x 2 would be possible solutions).

Shuffling/dealing

Pupils could play a card game with only the number cards. This gives them 36 cards to play with. When pupils deal out the cards, instead of piling them they could make an array e.g. if there are 4 players the array would need 4 rows; for 6 players there would be 6 rows. 36 can be arranged in a number of different arrays so this suits different numbers of players: 2, 3, 4, 6, 9, 12, 18 players can all have cards without any left over. Playing cards used in this way is also a very useful way of introducing or reinforcing the idea of remainders.

The array is also very powerful for showing how grouping and sharing are related.

36 ÷ 4 can be thought of in two different ways:

- Grouping: How many groups of 4 are there in 36?
- Sharing: How many in each set if 36 is split into 4 groups?

Imagine this set of 36 cubes is to be divided by 4. We can either think of it as **sharing**: split into 4 rows, so the answer would be 9 in each, or we can think of it as **grouping**: counting groups of 4, so the answer would be 9 groups in total. This can be enhanced by using mini-figures. How can we share 36 cards between 4 people or how many people can get 4 cards?

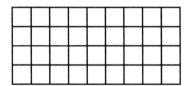

Inverse operations (division and multiplication)

Just as it is important to understand subtraction and addition in relation to one another, so division and multiplication should be learned together. 3 x 12 = ? and ? x 12 = 36 are puzzles based on the same calculation with one piece of information hidden from each. A simple diagram can help pupils visualise this idea. We will call these IMD Triangles (Inverse Multiplication and Division Triangles):

$$\begin{array}{c} \square \\ \div \quad \div \\ \square \times \square \end{array}$$

$$\begin{array}{c} \square \\ \div \quad \div \\ 4 \times 7 \end{array}$$

$$4 \times 7 = \square$$

$$\square \div 4 = 7$$

$$\begin{array}{c} 32 \\ \div \quad \div \\ 16 \times \square \end{array}$$

$$16 \times \square = 32$$

$$32 \div 16 = \square$$

The diagrams link multiplication and division. The product is placed at the top of the triangle and the two multipliers are placed at the base. Whichever piece of information is missing can be calculated using the other two corners of the triangle. Once pupils understand how the calculations match the diagrams, they can use it to help organise their thinking when they have to solve any problem involving multiplication and division e.g. given the word problem, pupils can use division triangles for different steps:

60 pupils want to visit the beach.

Type of bus	Number of pupil seats	Cost of hire
Mini-bus	12	£30 per day
Coach	30	£72 per day

Which type of bus is the cheapest to hire for their trip?

$$60 \div \div 12 \times \square$$

$12 \times 2 = 24$
$12 \times 4 = 48$
$12 \times 5 = 60$

5 minibuses needed!

This shows how the IMD triangles can be used to support thinking during problem solving. Here, the working shows that the missing number multiplies by 12 to make 60. A few trials shown on the left hand side soon find the answer: 5.

Quick activity: Yellow card!

For this you need only a blank sheet of yellow card. The aim of this activity is to help pupils understand that the blank card just symbolises a rectangle and that it is NOT TO SCALE. (This will be a very important skill to grasp. In exams, diagrams are often not to scale and pupils frequently make errors by estimating or measuring the diagram as if it were).

Explain that you are going to give pupils some measurements and they will have to work out the missing measurements based on what you tell them. Agree beforehand on some terminology: Width (W), Height (H) and Area (A)

What is the AREA if:	What is the HEIGHT if:	What is the WIDTH if:	How many solutions can you find if you only know the area:
W = 10cm H = 5cm?	W = 10cm A = 50cm²?	H = 30cm A = 90cm²?	A = 56cm²
W = 5cm H = 10cm?	W = 5cm A = 50cm²?	H = 3cm A = 90cm²?	A = 560m²
W = 11cm H = 5cm?	W = 1cm A = 50cm²?	H = 30cm A = 900cm²?	A = 24cm²
W = 11 miles H = 4 miles?	W = 100cm A = 500cm²?	H = 300cm A = 900cm²?	A = 120miles²
W = 60m H = 5m?	W = 50cm A = 500cm²?	H = 30cm A = 9000cm²?	
W = 30m H = 10m?	W = 25cm A = 500cm²?	H = 15cm A = 9000cm²?	

To develop this activity further you can ask more open questions:

- What happens to the area you can see if I fold it in half? And then half again?
- What areas can you have if the width is double the height?
- Can you invent two different measurements for every area up from 1cm² up to 20cm²?
- If I tell you that the area is an odd number between 30 and 40 and that the width and the height are whole numbers, what different measurements could there be?
- If the width and the height are decimal numbers is the area also a decimal?

You can also introduce smaller pieces of card, perhaps blue and yellow. Hold up the blue in front of the yellow, and give the measurements. Pupils have to work out how much yellow they can see in different arrangements.

Multiplication chains

Presented with a calculation like 2 x 17 x 5, many pupils have a tendency to work from left to right and end up with a tricky calculation: 2 x 17 = 34 as the first step; 34 x 5 as the second. This can be greatly simplified for pupils based on the property of COMMUTATIVITY – the rule which means that 17 x 5 is the same as 5 x 17. Again, arrays are a really strong visual cue for comprehending commutativity. Once pupils feel confident with this, they can manipulate the expression 2 x 17 x 5 until it looks like 2 x 5 x 17. Now, it is clear that this simplifies to 10 x 17 which can be calculated simply. Pupils might like to think of this as a kind of 'secret trick' but it is based on sound mathematics and encourages flexible thinking. They can practise with a number of variations:

2 x 19 x 5	4 x 19 x 5	2 x ? x 5 = 390
5 x 23 x 2	5 x 23 x 4	? x 16 x 2 = 160
2 x 31 x 5	4 x 31 x 5	? x 16 x 5 = 320
5 x 73 x 2	5 x 73 x 4	4 x ? x 5 = 700
5 x 9 x 2	5 x 9 x 4	5 x 17 x ? = 340
2 x 3.5 x 5	4 x 3.5 x 5	? x 17 x 5 = 3400

As we have seen in a number of activities, variation within and across an exercise can be used to draw out pattern and mathematical thinking.

Investigation: 10 cube challenge

Give pupils 10 cubes or 10 counters in a row.

Pupils have to split the cubes into chunks (akin to the partitioning activity):

This will give a chain of numbers to multiply together:

3 x 5 x 2 = 30.

There are a number of different avenues of exploration for this activity:

- How many different ways can the cubes be split to give an answer of 30?
- What's the maximum total that can be made in this way?
- Which numbers can be made in this way and which can't?
- How many different totals can be made by splitting the cubes into 2 chunks? What about 3 chunks?
- How many different square numbers can you make using cube chunks?
- Can you make all the numbers 1–20 in this way?
- How confident can you be that you have found all the possibilities?

Once pupils have had a chance to explore 10 cubes, they can investigate for a different number of cubes.

- What totals are possible for 4/5/6 cubes?
- Is the maximum for 8 cubes double the maximum for 4 cubes?
- Can you get a total of greater than 1000 using 20 cubes?
- What is the smallest number of cubes that can give you a score greater than 20? 30? 100?

Grid method

The grid method has been popular amongst some teachers in recent years because it is a natural progression from arrays. The grid method can be taught as a way of representing large arrays efficiently. It can easily be used for multiplication involving decimals and fractions. Also, because it builds on a property called associativity (which means that 5 x (3+2) = 5 x 3 + 5 x 2), the method can be adapted for multiplying algebraic expressions later in pupils' mathematical study. However, if it is taught merely as a process without understanding and awareness of how it works then it can seem like a long-winded drawing exercise.

> **Investigation: Vast arrays**
>
> Create a number of large arrays using the table function on a word processor or a spreadsheet. Challenge pupils to find a quick way to show how to count the squares in the arrays.

Here is a 32 by 7 array:

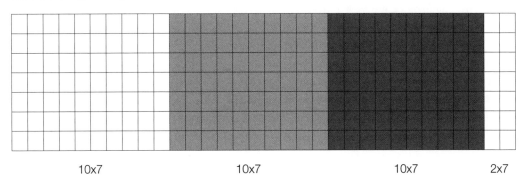

| 10x7 | 10x7 | 10x7 | 2x7 |

This array has been split into blocks 10 columns wide because these are easy to calculate with. A little working out shows that 32 x 7 = 70 + 70 + 70 + 14. Challenge pupils to find other ways of breaking up the calculation. Do they all come to the same answer?

Pupils can investigate a number of different arrays using highlighter pens or colouring pencils to mark out the different blocks. Challenge pupils to draw a VLA (Very Large Array) of their own. They will soon find out it is a laborious task. Perhaps we can come up with a way of representing the arrays by drawing diagrams that are not to scale:

	16	
4	10 x 4	6 x 4

The above array shows 16 x 4. After pupils have become well versed in representing arrays like this, they can move on to ELA (Even Larger Arrays) such as 27 x 13 as shown below.

	27	
13	20 x 10	7 x 10
	3 x 20	3 x 7

Challenge pupils to invent an array that is split into 3 or 6 blocks. Use this as an opportunity to assess how well they have linked the idea of place value and partitioning and the structure of the calculation. By developing the diagram from arrays, pupils should be encouraged to see how the grid method is a representation of the multiplication rather than merely as a procedure to be followed to get an answer.

Flexible partitioning

If we look a bit more closely at the grid method it becomes apparent that it too relies on an idea of flexible partitioning, of splitting the numbers up into parts that suit the calculation. Pupils should have the sense that they can take apart the numbers and put them back together, deciding how to make the calculation more efficient and clear. Once pupils can use the grid method with some accuracy they can try to break it. Think of it as the same as young children exploring their toys!

They might start to think that you have to partition the numbers into hundreds, tens and units to be able to perform the calculations. But look at these grid methods, and see what you notice:

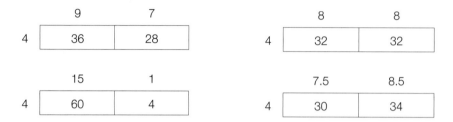

In every case, 16 x 4 works out as 64. It appears that however you partition 16, if you perform accurate multiplications, the result always comes out the same. Adventurous pupils might even like to try partitioning 16 into 17 and -1, or 20 and -4, or 2000.1 and -1984.1. Providing as the constituent calculations are accurate, the partitioning can be as you like.

Investigation: Double digits

This follows on from 'Beat the calculator' (page 11). Pupils will need a calculator to begin with.

Introduction

Ask pupils to choose a 2-digit number, perhaps 27, and type it into their calculator. They then have to multiply their number by 1010101. What do they notice? Their read-out should say 27272727, if they chose 27. Now they can try multiplying 1010101 by a few more 2-digit numbers. Pupils should notice that their original number repeats four times in the answer.

● What happens if they multiply 1010101 by a 1-digit number? What about a 3-digit number?

Development

The main part of the lesson will be about trying to work out why the pattern exists and how to adapt it. Begin with a couple of simplifications:

101 x 27 and 101 x 72

If we look at 101, we can partition it into 100 and 1. We can then multiply it using a written method:

	100	1
27	2700	27

```
  2  7  0  0
+       2  7
_____
  2  7  2  7
```

Notice how when we use these grids, we have partitioned them for ease of use rather than slavishly splitting everything into hundreds tens and units.

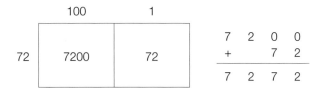

	100	1
72	7200	72

```
  7 2 0 0
+     7 2
---------
  7 2 7 2
```

Of course, the same calculations can be performed using a different method. The important thing is to look for why the repeated patterns occur. The pupils should try out a few of their own 101 multiplications to draw out the structure of the digits. Once they have become confident with the pattern they can investigate what happens when you multiply a 1-digit or 3-digit number by 101.

Progression

- What do the multiplication workings look like for x10101 or x1010101?
- Can you invent calculations to produce 7272727272, 31313131313131 or 909090909090909090909090?
- What happens when you multiply a number by 1001? What about 1001001? Can you find different levels of repeating digits?
- Can you invent a calculation that produces the answer 987 654 321 987 654 321?
- What happens when you multiply a number by 1.01 or 1.0101?

These exercises should demonstrate that what is important is understanding how the grid method can be used efficiently to build an understanding of how multiplications can be solved. The pupil who understands how arrays, the grid method, column multiplication and other methods are all linked will be far better placed to apply any of these methods efficiently and accurately.

Column multiplication

Column multiplication relies on the same idea as the grid method, that 25 x 17 can be split up into smaller operations: (25 x 10) + (25 x 7). A very common misconception is to think that you multiply the tens by the tens, and the units by the units, akin to column addition.

Discussion point

Because the column method does not require drawing of boxes and can be written quite compactly, some people consider it superior to other methods. Discuss the following statements:

- Calculators are quicker than people.
- Calculators never make a mistake.
- The most important thing is to get the exact right answer.
- Humans are better at maths than computers.

- The hardest part is understanding what to do to solve a problem.

- The best mathematicians are the ones who can do the hardest calculations.

Pupils will have opinions on these issues and it will be a revealing way to judge the general attitude to maths in the class. Many pupils will think that the way to get better at maths is to do calculations with larger numbers. Use the above statements to open up discussion about problem solving and using calculation methods effectively.

There are a number of variations of column multiplication depending on how people keep track of the digits that carry over. Look at the alternative approaches to the calculation below and see if you can decipher the workings and how they relate. Any of these, or none, might seem more intuitively helpful to a pupil.

```
   217              217                217
 × 38             × 38               × 38
─────            ─────                 5
 1686              56               ─────
 6310              80               1686
 125             1600                 2
  1              210                6310
─────             300                11
 8246            6000               ─────
                 ───                8246
                  11
                 ────
                 8246
```

There are alternative ways of breaking down the stages in column multiplication and different positions to record carried digits. Pupils will need to understand how the calculation method works to be able to use the method accurately.

Pupils need time to practise column multiplication with a purpose, rather than simply performing calculation after calculation without engaging their brains. Below are some questions with time as the context:

- How many minutes in a day?

- How many hours in a year?

- How many seconds in 4 months?

- How many seconds are you at school in a day?

- How many minutes are there in a school week?

- How long is your favourite film in minutes?

Another good way to give pupils the chance to practise meaningfully is to display calculations with a deliberate error in each. If pupils have to spot and understand the error then they will learn more than simply working out the right answer.

Long and short division

It is quite likely that the majority of pupils in your class will think division is the trickiest calculation to perform. However, in the work already discussed in this chapter about grouping and sharing, and on multiplication and division inverse triangles, much of the groundwork has already been done.

Discussion point: Division vocabulary

Before working on division, it will be important to agree some specific vocabulary to enable accurate and meaningful discussion e.g.

$$32 \div 4 = 8$$

Dividend = the number you are dividing. (In the example: 32)
Divisor = the number you are dividing *by*. (In the example: 4)
Quotient = the result of the calculation. (In the example: 8)

Both long and short division work on the idea of partitioning. Look at the example of long division given below:

```
          2   6   4
      ┌─────────────
    3 │ 7   9   2
          6   0   0
      ─────────────
          1   9   2
          1   8   0
      ─────────────
              1   2
              1   2
```

It is worth noting a few key points:

- Unlike addition and subtraction, the process works from left to right, from the higher place value to the lower.
- At each stage the remainder is shifted right. This is a little like the idea of carrying or exchanging in addition and subtraction.
- It can be thought of as grouping – how many groups of the divisor can be made out of the value being considered?

Short division, sometimes called 'The Bus-Stop' method, uses the same process but collapses the steps even further.

```
          2   6    4
      ┌──────────────
    3 │ 7   ¹9   ¹2
```

In both short and long division the process hinges on pupils being able to understand what to do with remainders, both during the process and at the end.

Investigation: Understanding remainders

A good way to improve pupils' performance at division calculation is to increase their confidence with remainders. Below are a number of questions that can be used regularly to prompt discussion and to identify misconceptions:

- Can you work out a number that has a remainder of 1 when you divide it by 10?
- Can you give me a list of numbers that all have a remainder of 1 when you divide by 10? What do you notice?
- How many numbers less than 50 give a remainder of 2 when you divide by 5?
- I am thinking of a number. When you divide it by 3 it gives a remainder of 1, and when you divide it by 4 it gives a remainder of 2. What could it be? How many solutions can you find?
- Can you think of 5 numbers that give an even remainder when you divide by 4? Can you think of any numbers that give an even remainder when you divide by 2? What do you notice?
- How do I know that the remainder from $365 \div 7$ can't possibly be 12? Is there a general rule here?
- What is the remainder from $4 \div 5$? (Note – this does not mean 5 divided by 4.)
- What is the remainder from $4 \div 10$? What about $4 \div 1\,000\,000$? Why is the remainder 4 every time? Can you think of how to explain this rule in words?

Alternative methods

There are a huge number of different calculation methods. Perhaps more important than the methods themselves is the fact that **all the methods produce the same answer**, providing the underlying mathematics is sound. At the heart of any calculation method is a way of breaking up the problem into smaller steps and then recombining the results for a final answer. Very often the mathematics hinges on the idea of flexible partitioning or of commutativity. Below are some examples of methods that pupils may enjoy researching.

Investigation: Alternative calculation methods

Double, double, double

Take any number. Double it, then double the answer. Now double the answer again.
For example, if you pick 13 you get:

$13 \rightarrow 26 \rightarrow 52 \rightarrow 104$

Now work out 13 x 8. You should find that 13 x 8 = 104.

In fact, double double double will multiply any number by 8.

Try it on several numbers, and check the answers using a calculator. Why does this work? Can you think of a similar trick for x16, or x4? How many doubles would you have to do to multiply a number by 64?

Binary multiplication

Choose a number you want to multiply, say 17. Now work out a series of doubles:

$$1 \times 17 = 17$$
$$2 \times 17 = 34$$
$$4 \times 17 = 68$$
$$8 \times 17 = 136$$
$$16 \times 17 = 272$$
$$32 \times 17 = 544$$

Now, if you want to multiply 17 by 12 you can find 4 x 17 and 8 x 17 and add them together: 12 x 17 = 68 + 136

You may need to add more than two numbers to find the multiplication you want e.g. 7 x 17 is (4 x 17) + (2 x 17) + (1 x 17) = 68 + 34 + 17 = 119.

This is how computers work out multiplications. It is a very efficient method that can work for any number and requires only doubling and adding. Challenge pupils to discover how it works, based on flexible partitioning.

Napier's bones

This is a method for multiplication that uses boxes divided diagonally. It can be a very quick and efficient way of performing large multiplications. Many examples are available on the internet. Pupils could research the method with their teacher or an adult supervisor. They could try to work out how the method works then present it to the class.

4
Decimals and Fractions

Key concept

The activities in this book are not exhaustive but they should enable pupils and teachers to build a sense of empowerment. Anyone undertaking calculations should feel that the numbers are under their control and that they can adapt methods to suit different calculations. In this chapter we will look at the modifications pupils can make to enable them to work fluently with decimals and fractions as well as whole numbers.

Common decimal misconceptions

Most of the calculation methods discussed so far work for decimals with very little modification but there are some very common misconceptions that pupils develop as they attempt to generalise their thinking.

Common error	Prompts and solutions
2.5 + 2.03 = 4.8	This comes from a lack of understanding of place value after the decimal place. Encourage pupils to understand that 2.5 = 2.50 = 2.500 = 2.500000000. . . This can also be remedied if pupils understand that the place value columns must be lined up in columns: <table><tr><td></td><td>T</td><td>U</td><td>•</td><td>1/10</td><td>1/100</td><td>1/1000</td></tr><tr><td></td><td></td><td>2</td><td>•</td><td>5</td><td></td><td></td></tr><tr><td>+</td><td></td><td>2</td><td>•</td><td>0</td><td>3</td><td></td></tr><tr><td></td><td></td><td>4</td><td>•</td><td>5</td><td>3</td><td></td></tr></table>
3.2 + 0.1 = 3.2.1	This error demonstrates that pupils have not understood what the decimal point signifies. In fact, it is nothing more than a signal that the digit on its left is to be read as the units digit.
10 x 3.5 = 30.5	Here, pupils see the decimal point as a block past which digits may not move. Demonstrate how when you multiply or divide by 10, 100, 1000 and so on, that the digits are linked and no other digit may split them up. This can be done with pupils linking arms, and moving to the left and the right, as a way of understanding the movement.

Common error	Prompts and solutions
2.5 x 10 = 2.50	Here, pupils have developed a general rule along the lines of: 'When you multiply by 10 you just *add* a zero'. This is very common, and understandable. Pupils need to see that each digit shifts one place, as a 5 becomes 50, a 90 becomes 900 and so on.
25 ÷ 0.1 = 2.5	There are interesting results for multiplying and dividing by 0.1. Encourage pupils to try a range of these calculations on a calculator and then discuss what they notice. In fact, multiplying by 0.1 is the same as dividing by 10, and dividing by 0.1 is the same as multiplying by 10. These interesting results should provoke some fascinating hypotheses and detailed discussion.
0.5 x 0.4 = 2.0	This may come from a sense that when you multiply, numbers should grow. In fact, pupils should come to see that when you multiply by a number less than 1, the resulting effect will be a reduction rather than an enlargement.

We can adapt the use of variation to help pupils develop fluency in their understanding of calculations with decimals.

Variation for decimal multiplication			
7 x 100 = ?	7 x 200 = ?	0.7 x ? = 0.7	7 x ? = 2.8
7 x 10 = ?	7 x 20 = ?	7 x ? = 0.7	70 x ? = 2.8
7 x 1 = ?	7 x 2 = ?	70 x ? = 0.7	700 x ? = 2.8
7 x 0.1 = ?	7 x 0.2 = ?	700 x ? = 0.7	7000 x ? = 2.8
7 x 0.01 = ?	7 x 0.02 = ?	? x 70 = 7	7 x ? = 2.8
7 x 0.001 = ?	7 x 0.002 = ?	? x 700 = 7	7 x ? = 0.28
			7 x ? = 0.028

Decimal remainders

A simple adaptation of short (or 'Bus-Stop') division opens up the method for decimal remainders. The trick is to notice that you can write as many zeros on to the right hand side of a number and the number remains the same:

12.3 = 12.30 = 12.300 = 12.3000000000 . . .

Once that is in place, you can use short division very simply with decimals and produce answers with as many decimal places as you like. The key, as with adding and subtracting decimals, is to make sure that the decimal points line up.

$$
\begin{array}{r|ccccccccc}
 & & & & \bullet \\
8 & 3 & 3 & 5 & \bullet & 0 & 0 & 0 & 0 \\
\hline
 & 0 & 4 & 1 & \bullet & 8 & 7 & 5 \\
\hline
8 & 3 & {}^33 & {}^15 & \bullet & {}^70 & {}^60 & {}^40 & 0 \\
\end{array}
$$

Once pupils have understood how to use decimal remainders they can investigate some interesting number patterns. There is a common mistake when trying to do divisions like 4 ÷ 9. It is similar to a mistake often made with subtraction. We nearly always encounter division where the number we divide by (the divisor) is smaller than the number we are dividing (the dividend). When pupils see something like 4 ÷ 9, they frequently assume it means 9 ÷ 4, just written differently. The activity below tackles that misconception and demonstrates the link between decimals and fractions.

Investigation: Decimal remainder patterns

Starter

Pupils can try these divisions using short division as a starter. Model how they will need to include zeros after the decimal points and how they need to take care over which number is the dividend (the number being divided) and the divisor (the number you are dividing by). Each of these sequences will produce a pattern of digits. Once pupils have spotted the pattern for each, encourage them to predict the next in the sequence and then check the result.

1 ÷ 4	1 ÷ 5	1 ÷ 9	1 ÷ 11	1 ÷ 3
2 ÷ 4	2 ÷ 5	2 ÷ 9	1 ÷ 11	1 ÷ 6
3 ÷ 4	3 ÷ 5	3 ÷ 9	1 ÷ 11	1 ÷ 12
4 ÷ 4	4 ÷ 5	4 ÷ 9	1 ÷ 11	1 ÷ 24
5 ÷ 4	. . .	. . .	. . .	. . .
. . .				

Development

Now, pupils should have an idea of recurring decimals. Teach how to use notation.
Place a dot over the repeating digit: 0.33333. . . = 0.$\dot{3}$

If there is more than one digit in the repeating pattern, such as 0.3636363636, then place a dot over the first and last repeating digit e.g. 0.$\dot{3}\dot{6}$ or a line over the repeating pattern e.g. 0.$\overline{36}$
Based on what they have discovered, challenge pupils to find divisions with these answers:

> 4.33333. . .
> 11.25
> 8.8
> 9.11111. . ...
> 9.18181818. . .

Further challenges:

- Invent decimal answers for a partner to create a division.

- Look at the pattern when you divide by 7. Do the digits repeat?

- Which of these do you predict will create recurring decimals? ÷8, ÷13, ÷25, ÷14, ÷99, ÷500?

- Try these calculations on a calculator. What happens to some of the recurring decimals on a calculator display?

Fraction calculations

$$\frac{1}{2} + \frac{1}{3} = ?$$

Learning to calculate with fractions is more complicated than with decimals. Even calculations as seemingly simple as a half plus a third is fraught with potential misconceptions. It is vital that pupils develop a sound understanding of fractions: of shapes, of amounts, as percentages, as operators, as numbers in their own right. To explore the topic in depth would be the subject of a whole book. In terms of the four operations there are a number of 'good habits' that pupils can practise to help prevent misconceptions:

Addition and subtraction of fractions

In fact, addition and subtraction of fractions is probably the trickiest skill to understand and perform. The key is to comprehend:

- Why the denominators must be made equal before adding and subtracting; and
- Why we only add or subtract the numerators.

It would be perfectly reasonable to expect that:

$$\frac{1}{2} + \frac{1}{3} = \frac{2}{5}$$

Why should this not be true?

A good way to start to demonstrate this is with arrays and the trick is to pick an array that can be split into halves and thirds. This can be done by splitting the array into halves horizontally and thirds vertically:

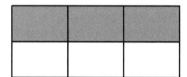 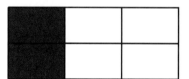

Now, we can see that $\frac{3}{6}$ is a half, and $\frac{2}{6}$ is a third. To add these two quantities, we can imagine combining them into one array:

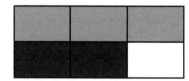

This gives us $\dfrac{5}{6}$ so the calculation looks like:

$$\frac{1}{2} + \frac{1}{3} = \frac{3}{6} + \frac{2}{6} = \frac{5}{6}$$

The use of arrays is one way of ensuring that pupils begin to build a visual intuition and understanding of how fractions are combined through addition and subtraction.

To follow this, look at:

$$\frac{1}{2} - \frac{1}{3} = ?$$

Using our arrays from above, we can see that this is equivalent to $\dfrac{3}{6}$ subtract $\dfrac{2}{6}$. Some exploration of arrays will soon turn up the answer!

Multiplication and division of fractions

Because fractions are built on proportional relationships, they behave a little better under multiplication and division.

Problem solving: Folding fractions!

Give each pupil 4 rectangles of scrap paper and explain that although they appear to be scrap, they are in fact very expensive pieces of high quality parchment. Challenge pupils to fold each piece into fractions:

- Fold the first piece in half;
- The next into quarters;
- Fold the next into thirds;
- And the final piece into eighths.

Folding into thirds will be approximate. Encourage pupils to think of this as representative. Get them to aim for accuracy but accept that there is some guesswork and measuring by eye. All of the others can be done exactly. On each piece they should write the fraction. The folded quarters will look like:

¼	¼
¼	¼

Now explain that because it is very expensive parchment, each sheet costs £24. Pupils can then work out the cost of each fraction by performing the relevant division. Write the cost of each fraction on the parchment.

¼ £6	¼ £6
¼ £6	¼ £6

Now, pupils will be able to see how to find $\frac{3}{4}$ of £24, by combining the cost of three $\frac{1}{4}$ sections. Since, $\frac{1}{4}$ of £24 costs £6, the cost of $\frac{3}{4}$ will be 3 x £6 = £18. They can then work out a number of different fractions of £24 by looking at their folded fractions and finding the correct amounts to multiply.

As a follow-up, pupils can draw diagrams for different fractions of different amounts (rather than folding all that expensive parchment!).

For example:

- Draw a diagram to show $\frac{2}{5}$ of £40

- Draw a rectangle to show how to find $\frac{5}{12}$ of £72

This technique can be used to help pupils build an understanding of how to find any fraction of any amount by dividing by the denominator and multiplying by the numerator.

Fractions and division

In fact, fractions and division are deeply interlinked.

Discussion point: Division symbol

Look closely at the division symbol.

$\div$

- It is a curious symbol. Why is it written like that?
- What could the line represent? What about the dots?
- Is it possible that the dots represent the numerator and denominator of a fraction?
- Why would the symbol for division look so like a fraction?

Some pupils might like to research the operator symbol for division and to find out the names for its various parts. It is a clue about how division and fractions are linked.

Mathematicians rarely use the division symbol. If ever they want to write '9 divided by 4' they simply write it as a fraction: $\frac{9}{4}$.

Starting to think of division like this leads to a very simple division method that uses fractions and flexible partitioning. We can use 364 ÷ 7 to demonstrate. We know that we want to divide the number 364 by 7, so we can write it as a fraction:

$$\frac{364}{7}$$

Next we will partition the numerator into parts that suit our calculation. Since we are dividing by 7 we want parts that divide nicely by 7. A little thought gives 350 + 14. Now we can write our fraction as:

$$\frac{350}{7} + \frac{14}{7}$$

The two parts can be worked out separately:

$$\frac{350}{7} = 50, and \ \frac{14}{7} = 2$$

Which leaves us with the answer 52. So $364 \div 7 = 52$.

Below are some further examples of this method. Although it looks like complex mathematics, it is really very efficient and elegant. Pupils should only learn this method once they are confident in using equivalent fractions but it is a very good method that will help them as they progress through algebra. It also gives a very clear way of understanding fractional remainders.

$$92 \div 4 = \frac{80}{4} + \frac{12}{4} = 20 + 3 = 23$$

$$93 \div 4 = \frac{80}{4} + \frac{12}{4} + \frac{1}{4} = 20 + 3 + \frac{1}{4} = 23\frac{1}{4}$$

$$192 \div 4 = \frac{100}{4} + \frac{80}{4} + \frac{12}{4} = 25 + 20 + 3 = 48$$

$$8293 \div 4 = \frac{8000}{4} + \frac{200}{4} + \frac{80}{4} + \frac{12}{4} + \frac{1}{4} = 2000 + 50 + 20 + 3 + \frac{1}{4} = 2073\frac{1}{4}$$

Further mathematical thinking

This section contains a range of ideas for how to apply the skills of calculation in various mathematical contexts. There are some very interesting patterns in number, and we can extend pupils' appreciation dramatically.

Very Interesting Patterned numbers (VIP numbers):

- Palindromic numbers: 12321, 3443, 6724276
- Consecutive numbers: 23, 24, 25 199, 200, 201, 202
- Rising numbers (digits increase): 1234, 345678, 123456789
- Very large numbers: millions, billions, trillions, quadrillions, quintillions, . . .

- Powers of two: 2, 4, 8, 16, 32, 64, 128, 256...
- Triangular numbers: 1, 3, 6, 10, 15, ...
- Square Numbers: 1, 4, 9, 16, 25, ...
- Fibonacci Numbers: 1, 1, 2, 3, 5, 8, 13, ...

Picking a kind of patterned number to explore and investigate will strengthen pupils' understanding of how the numbers fit together rather than behaving like a sea of random digits.

Quick activity: Patterned calculations

If you want to give your class some calculation practice at the beginning or end of a lesson or as an exercise, then choose a pattern for all the numbers rather than picking at random.

For example:

Triangle building blocks	Square differences	Powers of two
1 + 2 + 3 + 4	4–1	2 x 4
11 + 12 + 13 + 14	9 – 4	4 x 16
101 + 102 + 103 + 104	16 – 9	128 ÷ 4
	25 – 16	256 ÷ 32
	. . .	
How can knowing the answer to the first calculation help find the other answers?	Subtract a square number from the next square number (you will get the odd numbers as answers).	Multiply or divide a power of two by a power of two (you will always end up with another power of two).

Pupils will be hooked by the structure and will enjoy 'cracking the code'. It also allows for comparison between results e.g. how are 1 + 2 + 3 + 4 and 101 + 102 + 103 + 104 related? If pupils get used to the fact that calculations come in families, then they will start to think of how they can use one fact to find others and use one thing they know to solve something that seems unfamiliar.

Always, sometimes, never true

These categories of number make excellent subjects for a well-known style of activity called 'Always, sometimes, never'. Pupils are given a statement and they have to decide if it is always true, sometimes true or never true. When pupils are required to *investigate specific examples*, make and *justify their decisions* and then *think of their own* statements, they will be going through the same process as professional mathematicians and engaged in a very high level of mathematical thinking. This activity should not be rushed nor underestimated and can be adapted for a range of topics. 'Always, sometimes, never' tasks can be set up very easily. The main preparation will be pre-teaching the vocabulary pupils will need to interpret the statements.

The activity described below uses consecutive numbers for a context but it can be adapted for use with any of the VIP numbers described above. Should the pupils be allowed to use calculators? It depends what you want from the activity:

- Allow calculators if you want to focus on the reasoning and on using patterns to guide a line of enquiry.
- Do not allow calculators if you want pupils to practise calculation methods in a mathematical context.

Both approaches are perfectly valid and you can adapt as suits your pupils and suits your needs.

Investigation: Always, sometimes, never true: consecutive numbers

Setting up and organisation

Pre-teach vocabulary – this can be done before the lesson, before break or even the day before (but no earlier). For consecutive numbers, a visual cue such as a number track or a 100 square will help. Finding a simple definition to rehearse is also important: consecutive numbers are 'a group of numbers one after the other', 'a group of counting numbers in order', 'numbers that go up in ones'.

To practise, play a game of consecutive bingo. Use 3 x 3 bingo grids. Pupils have to make every row have three consecutive numbers. They win if they get a row of three. To win, they have to be able to tell you that what their consecutive numbers were, e.g. "I chose the consecutive numbers: 23, 24 and 25."

Lesson flow

Engagement
Write the following statement on the board:

'Consecutive numbers are next to each other on a 100 square.'

If your class enjoy arguing their case, you can engage the pupils by saying: "I'm the teacher, and I'm ALWAYS right." Write down a list of numbers that 'prove' you are always right or use a large version of a 100 square: 24 and 25, 36 and 37, 95 and 96. . . Wait for a pupil to point out that there are some instances where it doesn't work (where the first number is on the end of a row).

List all the examples where you were wrong and model how to back down graciously: "OK. So, I'm the teacher and I am SOMETIMES right."

Enquiry
Choose three statements from the table given on page 100. These can be displayed on the board for all to see or distributed to pupils depending on their understanding. Challenge pupils to try a number of examples to test out if the statements are always, sometimes, or never true. Encourage pupils to go beyond just a few examples. If they have a narrow approach then they may miss some important results.

Development
Once pupils have a number of examples, encourage them to organise the results and look for patterns. The following questions will push their understanding further:

- Can you write an instruction for how to produce examples that support this statement?
- How could you change this statement so that it becomes always true?
- Can you compare statements? Are any of your statements more true than others?

Plenary

Use these sentence starters to prompt pupils to think of their own statements:

- When you add two even numbers, . . .
- When you multiply an even number by 5 . . .
- If you take away a multiple of 5 from a multiple of ten . . .

Next Steps

It is very difficult to come up with statements that are NEVER true. Can pupils think of any? Begin with a discussion of: "Lying is ok". Pupils will be able to think of plausible arguments why this may be true sometimes. If a heated debate starts up, then model how to listen to alternative opinions. What is important is that pupils feel they can use this activity to dig into the properties of a statement which is a very powerful mathematical tool.

Always, sometimes, never statements about consecutive numbers

The statements are given in two different styles. Judge which style your pupils will understand confidently. It is worth noticing how a technical style gets the information across with fewer words. A brief explanation of when they are true is given in the third column. For pupils, learning to explore in depth and reason for themselves will be more important than finding the right answer.

Technical style	Informal style	Always, sometimes, never
The sum of two consecutive numbers is odd.	When you add two consecutive numbers, you get an odd answer.	Always – it always involves adding an odd and an even, which always gives an odd result.
The product of two consecutive numbers is odd.	When you multiply two consecutive numbers, you get an odd answer.	Never – whenever you multiply an odd by an even, you get an even result.
The sum of three consecutive numbers is a multiple of 5.	When you add three consecutive numbers, you get an answer in the 5 times table.	Sometimes – if the middle number of the three is a multiple of 5.
The sum of consecutive numbers is even.	When you add some consecutive numbers, you get an even answer.	Sometimes – it depends on how many consecutive numbers you have chosen to sum.

Technical style	Informal style	Always, sometimes, never
The sum of consecutive numbers is 15.	You can make fifteen by adding consecutive numbers.	Sometimes – 4 + 5 + 6 = 15, and 7 + 8 = 15, but most results, such as 44 + 45 + 46 = 135.
The product of 3 consecutive numbers is a multiple of 10.	When you multiply 3 consecutive numbers together, you get a number in the 10 times table.	Sometimes – if one of the numbers is a multiple of 10 or a multiple of 5.
The product of consecutive numbers is odd.	When you multiply any consecutive numbers, you get an odd answer.	Never – there is always an even number in the multiplication, and so the result is always even.
It is possible to write a number as a sum of consecutive numbers in more than one way.	You can find more than one way of adding consecutive numbers to get the same answer.	Sometimes – there's only one way to write 6 as a sum of consecutives: 1 + 2 + 3, there are no ways of writing 12 as a sum of consecutives, but there are two ways of writing 15.

By using this style of activity, pupils will be thinking like professional mathematicians: thinking of reasons and generalities. This kind of thinking is what sets the human mind apart from the computer circuits that calculate at the speed of light. Humans are more than calculating machines, and for humans the 'why' is often more important than the 'how'.

Afterword

Taking a moment to revisit the book's definition of a creative approach to calculation, we can remind ourselves of three aims:

1. Developing a physical and visual intuition about number,
2. Encouraging pupils to forge links between their ideas and develop conceptual understanding,
3. Capturing pupils' curiosity and innate logical reasoning.

The activities in this book are designed to help pupils begin to see the patterns that make mathematics understandable, and even beautiful. Without the patterns, we really would have to learn every single fact off by heart, or carry with us a pocketful of pebbles everywhere we went, in case we needed to perform a calculation. The idea of 'variation' used to design sequences of calculations for pupils to practise is one simple way of bringing order out of chaos. Perhaps most important of all is the sense that the ideas are all interconnected. There is no 'right way' of solving a problem; one problem can be solved in a million different ways, by a million different people who had a million different breakfasts under a million different skies. The miracle is that each different method will produce the same answer, providing we follow the patterns built into the heart of mathematics.

If pupils gain an intuition about those patterns, begin to make connections between ideas, and become curious about how it all fits together and where their thinking might lead, then their innate logic will take them on a path of genuine mathematical discovery.